Stress is like the weather. Everyone talks about it, but no one does anything about it. That can change if you read this book and take its lessons to heart. The author is an expert in physical and psychology well-being, and she knows what she is talking about. Her good sense shows through on every page, and the book abounds with concrete suggestions not only about how to manage stress but more importantly about how to thrive. I highly recommend 10 Simple Solutions to Stress.

> —Christopher Peterson, Ph.D., professor of psychology and former director of clinical psychology training at the University of Michigan and author of *Character Strengths and Virtues* and *A Primer in Positive Psychology*

If Dr. Wheeler's 10 Simple Solutions to Stress *could be put into a pill, it would be prescribed in record numbers. This book teaches a set of skills that will substantially improve your quality of life and health. I will be recommending Dr. Wheeler's book to my patients and make it required reading for my medical students.*

> —Meg Hayes, MD, assistant professor of family medicine at Oregon Health and Science University

10 Simple Solutions to Stress

How to Tame Tension & Start Enjoying Your Life

CLAIRE MICHAELS WHEELER, MD, PH.D.

New Harbinger Publications, Inc.

Publisher's Note

This publication is designed to provide accurate and authoritative information in regard to the subject matter covered. It is sold with the understanding that the publisher is not engaged in rendering psychological, financial, legal, or other professional services. If expert assistance or counseling is needed, the services of a competent professional should be sought.

Spiritual Meaning Scale: Nathan Mascaro and David H. Rosen, *Journal of Humanistic Psychology* (volume 46, issue2) p. 178, copyright 2006 by Nathan Mascaro and David H. Rosen, reprinted by permission of Sage Publications, Inc.

COPE Questionnaire: Charles S. Carver, *International Journal of Behavioral Medicine* (volume 4) pp. 92–100, copyright 1997 by Charles S. Carver, reprinted by permission of Lawrence Erlbaum Associates.

Distributed in Canada by Raincoast Books

Library of Congress Cataloging-in-Publication Data

Wheeler, Claire Michaels.
  10 simple solutions to stress : how to tame tension and start enjoying your life / Claire Michaels Wheeler,MD, Ph.D.
      p. cm.
  ISBN-13: 978-1-57224-476-4
  ISBN-10: 1-57224-476-3
  1. Stress management. 2. Stress (Psychology) I. Title.
RA785.W45 2006
616.9'8—dc22

2006035214

08 07 06

10 9 8 7 6 5 4 3 2 1   First printing

This book is dedicated with love to my children: Elizabeth, Walker, and Jackson

Contents

Acknowledgments

I would like to acknowledge the people in my life who have supported and encouraged me along the way to having the privilege to write this book.

Chris Peterson, my dissertation advisor and friend at the University of Michigan—thank you for showing me how to think, research, and write about health and psychology from my own perspective and for encouraging me to develop originality and creativity in my work. James Gordon, the founder and director of the Center for Mind-Body Medicine, has been a mentor and guide since 1999, when I attended my first training with the center. Jim, thank you for believing in me even when I didn't. Joan Borysenko has been my role model for almost twenty years. Joan, thank you for your support and the beauty you bring into so many lives.

Everyone who ever came to see me at MindBody Medicine of Portland, who attended a workshop or joined a group—thank you. I've learned so much from you and your stories about the resiliency of the human spirit and what it means to thrive in the face of adversity. You inspire me to do the best work I can do.

My friends and colleagues have kept me going through good times and bad. Bonnie Comfort is the wisest woman I know and my most beloved friend. Hugs and kisses to Meg Hayes, Ruth Anderson, and Barbara Jensen for always being there. Special thanks to Susan Lord, Joel Evans, Bob Buckley, and the rest of the CMBM crew for making me a part of the tribe. Thanks to Leslie McBride for the work teaching at PSU.

I am very grateful to Tesilya Hanauer at New Harbinger Publications for promoting me as a new, untested author—for taking the time to talk with me and create ideas for this book. Jessica Beebe, my copyeditor, has been a joy to work with—thank you for making my words fit together so well.

Thanks to my mom, Sue Floyd, for setting an example of grace and humor under pressure. Thank you to my father, Herb Wheeler, who died in 1993, for always expecting the best from me when I was in school. Alex, Croix, and Levi—thank you for letting me be your friend and for all the fun we have together. Finally, I want to thank Matt for coming into my life. Your love makes my life richer, happier, and more peaceful. I love every moment I get to share with you.

Introduction

This book offers ten simple but powerful and creative ways to dramatically decrease the bad effects stress may be having in your life. Some of the results you'll see will be immediate—less muscle tension, clearer thinking, better sleep—and others will be like money in the bank. You'll be taking steps to make yourself less vulnerable to getting sick. You'll be making changes that could very well help you live a longer, happier, more fulfilling life.

You see, stress robs you of your very essence. It's like a thief in the night (literally, in the case of its effects on sleep) that creeps up on you gradually. Quite often, a person doesn't realize stress is an issue until it leads to symptoms like high blood pressure or chronic low back pain. Taking steps now to manage your stress levels can prevent such things from happening to you. And if you're already grappling with a medical condition, reducing stress can dramatically alter the course of your illness.

The health benefits of managing stress are legion, but there's another reason to do it. Clearing your body and mind of unnecessary stress and tension allows you to thrive. It makes room for creativity and spiritual growth, and frees you to pursue fun activities, build happier relationships, and truly appreciate the joy and vibrancy of your body. In short, getting control of stress allows you to focus on what's really important—finding meaning and joy in every day that you're lucky enough to be here on this earth.

I welcome you to this journey and encourage you to read with a sense of optimism. You can be happier, calmer, more focused, more loving, and healthier.

What Is Stress?

There has been great debate in the worlds of medicine, psychology, and sociology about the definition of stress. The word "stress" comes from the field of physics, where it refers to the amount of force applied to something. It's easy to see how that could apply to human experience. Traffic, interpersonal conflict, financial worries, job demands, health challenges: all of these exert force or pressure on your body, mind, and spirit. Some of this pressure comes from the environment, to be sure, but a surprising amount of it comes from inside your head, in the form of worry, regret, anxiety, and *ruminating* (literally "chewing" something over and over again).

So yes, stress is the force applied to you, but the real issue is the *strain* (another physics term) that occurs as a response to stress. What all stress management books, including this one, are really about is managing strain, or your responses to the challenges put in front of you all day every day, from within and from the environment. For some people, stress results in very little strain; they seem to thrive under pressure. For most of us, however, the stresses applied to us from every direction often leave us feeling unable to keep up, to cope, and to find satisfaction in the way we get things done. Many of us suffer from a sense of too little time and too much to do.

A HOLISTIC DEFINITION OF STRESS

The consensus now is that stress is a process—an interaction between the person and the environment. The working definition of stress, then, for most researchers and clinicians, is the situation that arises in you when life's challenges and pressures exceed your perceived ability to cope. Let's look at this definition closely. First, the situation that arises in a person: this is a physical, emotional, psychological, social phenomenon. In other words, it's a holistic response. Every part of you—body, mind, spirit, and relationships—is affected by the challenges of daily life. The good news is that each part of you can be called upon as a resource for managing these challenges. The second half of this definition of stress points to the importance of your perceived ability to cope. Coping is a skill that anyone can improve. Coping is the antidote to stress.

Stress and Coping

Stress involves a sequence of events, beginning with a threat. This threat may be real, like a deer running into the road in front of your car, or it may be a thought, like remembering that you forgot an important meeting that started two hours ago. Once you've evaluated the seriousness of the threat, the next step in the stress response is to evaluate your capability to handle it. This involves deciding how much, if any, control you have over the situation and your feelings about it, and how confident you are that you can respond capably to what has happened (or will happen).

In the case of the missed meeting, there are many possible ways to respond, depending on how much of a catastrophe you believe it was. Do you pace around, wringing your hands, trying to come up with a good excuse? Do you get angry and slam things around your office? Do you sit down and cry, feeling like you're never going to be able to manage all your responsibilities? Or maybe you pick up the phone, call someone who was at the meeting, and ask what you can do to catch up on what you missed. Each of these responses carries a price and a payoff. That's where coping comes in. Your job will be to develop the skills and confidence to choose wisely whenever you're presented with an opportunity to overcome the power of stress to hurt you.

There are different ways that people cope with stressors of all kinds, and some are clearly healthier than others. In chapter 2, you'll learn about your personal coping style. You'll identify which of your coping activities are helping you and which are creating more problems. You'll learn and practice better ways of reacting so when a challenge arises, you'll respond effectively, and when it's over, you'll be able to let it go.

Stress and Perception

Let's go back to the definition of stress as the situation that arises in you when life's challenges and pressures exceed your perceived ability to cope. The key is the emphasis on perception. How you assess a threat determines how your body, mind, and spirit will respond. In the case of the deer running in front of your car, instinct will probably take over and you'll do what's necessary to avoid hitting it. The meaning you ascribe to missing the meeting will determine how you respond to the situation. In fact, the meaning of everything that happens to you is entirely up to you.

Within the boundaries of normal human existence, stress is not what happens to you, it's what you think and feel about what happens to you. This means that you can control the amount of stress in your life. How?

- You can change what you think about what's going on around you.

- You can change how you react to what's going on around you.

- You can take charge of the fearful, worried, and anxious thoughts that plague your mind even when you're in a safe, comfortable situation.

- You can choose to avoid situations that create stress for you.

- You can choose to do things that create peace for you.

That's what this book is about. We'll explore ten simple solutions to the problem of stress, based on the power you have right now to change your thoughts, access your inner reserves of strength and vitality, learn new skills, and make new, healthy connections to the world around you.

ACUTE VS. CHRONIC STRESS

Generally speaking, there are two kinds of stress: acute and chronic. *Acute* (temporary) stress is useful; *chronic* (long-lasting) stress is less useful and can in fact be harmful.

The Acute Stress Response

The *acute stress response*, the immediate, automatic response to a stressful event, is one humans share with all other mammals. It's a survival mechanism that causes profound, nearly instantaneous changes in every body system. The general theme is *Danger! Run away!*

Imagine being a prey animal. All day long, you stand around and eat. Every now and then, a predator comes and kills one of the members of your herd. After the fleeing is over, you go back to eating. That's how your body and mind is meant to respond to threats in the environment. Recognize the threat, react effectively, calm down, learn from it, and get on with your life. Being able to have a beginning, middle, and end to your stress response is an extremely powerful way to manage life's crises, both big and small.

Immediately after you perceive a threat, your brain starts sending messages and releasing hormones that change your state from relaxed to red alert. Heart rate and blood pressure increase, and blood gets shunted away from your skin and digestive organs and into your brain and the large muscles of your body. All this helps you figure out where to run and gives you the leg power to do so.

Acute stress responses actually provide benefits to the body. In their recent article on the relationship between stress and aging, Louise Hawkley and her colleagues (2005) explained that having occasional acute stress responses actually helps immune function and builds resilience. A jolt of stress hormones every now and then keeps the immune system primed and ready to act in case of an injury or infection. It's important to realize that in managing stress, you're not aiming for a perennially serene, stress-free life (as if that were a realistic goal). You can think of acute stressors and your responses to them as a way of keeping you on your toes, ready to be strong when the going gets tough.

The acute stress response has two sources: the adrenal glands, which release the stress hormones *adrenaline* and *cortisol*, and the sympathetic nervous system. The *sympathetic nervous system* (SNS) originates in your brain and sends messages to nerve endings all over your body to create an instantaneous shift from a resting state to an alarm condition. It's the SNS that gets your heart pounding, your palms sweating, and your muscles tensed and ready to fight or flee in the first moment after a stressful thought or event occurs. You can think of the SNS as the fast-acting component of stress; the effects of the adrenal glands are more gradual and long-lasting.

The SNS can be stimulated, create its effects, and then return to a resting state in a few minutes, when the crisis is over. Whenever this happens, however, the adrenal glands become alerted and spurt out cortisol, which stays in your body for hours after the stressful trigger. If your day includes many small alarm reactions, over time these frequent SNS activations will cause the adrenal glands to maintain high levels of cortisol, which creates the physiology of chronic stress.

There's a vicious cycle at work here. Chronically elevated blood levels of cortisol can make your SNS more reactive to small and big stressors throughout the day. When your body and mind are in a state of chronic stress, even small triggers can stimulate a big acute stress response, perpetuating the cycle. With each SNS activation, you have a jump in blood pressure and heart rate, a shift of blood flow to your brain and big muscles, and a disruption of your ability to think clearly and rationally about what's going on. Over time, these changes can do damage to your health and peace of mind.

In addition to the noticeable physical changes with acute stress, there are important changes in the brain. Researcher Amy Arnsten (1998) of Yale University has found that during a strong stress reaction, the chemicals released cause a shift in the activity of the brain. The *amygdala*, a very primitive, instinctual region lying deep within the brain, becomes more active. This activation helps you make quick, survival-oriented decisions without being distracted by considering a lot of options. At the same time, the *prefrontal cortex*, where you do your thinking, assessing, and analyzing, becomes much less active.

Arnsten's research suggests that while the brain changes that happen in acute stress are helpful in simple, natural environments and in potentially violent encounters, they can work against you in more complex, modern situations. And when stress becomes chronic, it can cause significant problems with concentration, learning, and memory.

Chronic Stress

In the ideal world, once the threat has passed, all systems return to normal and you're able to relax. Your body was designed to do this automatically, but here's where we humans, with our big brains and vast imaginations, come into trouble. If you keep thinking about the threat—imagining all the terrible things that could have happened, what your friends would think, how much it would have cost, and on and on—you keep the threat alive. Images of catastrophe arise, seemingly out of your control. These images are interpreted by your body as real events. If you get stuck in threatened thinking, you get stuck in the stress response.

Have you ever met someone who is still angry about something that happened twelve years ago? Someone who experienced a tragic loss decades ago but is still grieving? Someone who blows up at the smallest glitch in the day's schedule? These are all signs that the acute, healthy stress response has been locked in the "on" position. The person can't get off the roller coaster. Most of the frustration, anger, sadness, and hopelessness you see in people around you (and in yourself) comes from being locked in to chronic stress.

Breaking the cycle of chronic stress starts in the here and now, not by delving into scars from the past. For some people, it's helpful to follow up with insight-oriented therapy to help make sense of the past. But for everyone, learning simple, effective ways to cope with stress right now is the best way to start.

What does it mean to live with chronic stress? Chronic stress affects the body and mind in different ways for every person. Some of what you notice has to do with your genetic makeup. Many symptoms of chronic stress, like lower back pain, run in families. Lifestyle also determines how stress shows up in the body. A person who tends to eat too quickly and chooses fatty, hard-to-digest foods may have more frequent episodes of stress-related heartburn and indigestion. Later in the book, you'll take a look at your own patterns of stress. You'll also assess your lifestyle for areas of vulnerability to the effects of stress.

THE PHYSICAL EXPERIENCE OF CHRONIC STRESS. In general, the physical symptoms of stress come from the effects of stress hormones on the various organs of the body. If you turn down the volume of the acute stress response, you get an idea of how chronic stress feels. People under chronic stress tend to have enhanced *cardiovascular reactivity*. This means that even in response to a minor upset, your heart races, your breath gets short, and you may feel sweaty and shaky. It may take longer than seems normal to calm down afterward. Other physical signs of chronic stress are muscle tension in the jaw, shoulders, or lower back. This can make it hard to work, relax, and simply feel good. Frequent headaches, fatigue, restlessness, and insomnia are more generalized symptoms of chronic stress.

Remember that you are unique and feel stress in your own way. In chapter 6, we'll look closely at how stress might be affecting you physically and what you can do to take better care of your body and counter the effects on all your body systems.

THE EMOTIONAL EXPERIENCE OF CHRONIC STRESS. Chronic stress is linked strongly with the two biggest psychological scourges of our time: depression and anxiety. The more stress you perceive in your life, the greater your likelihood of eventually being diagnosed with one of these conditions. Anxiety disorders are the most common mental disorders in the United States (Van Eck et al. 1996). They are a roller-coaster ride of tension, fatigue, and irritability.

The insidious thing about anxiety is that it's a response to thoughts, not to actual stressors. Fearful thoughts creep into waking life and dreams, and they trigger a stress response. This can happen over and over again, day in and day out. Anxiety is usually related to old, unconscious beliefs and ideas about life and self that, if brought to light, often don't even make sense. Stress management helps you stop the cycle of anxious thoughts and physiological responses so you can examine and dispose of these ideas.

Even without a diagnosable disorder, it's possible to have profound emotional discomfort as a result of stress. Chronic stress usually manifests as impatience and irritability. It can also feel like sadness and apathy. In more extreme cases, it can result in rage, which leads to bad behavior that's disruptive to relationships. It's not rare to hear family members report that a loved one's personality changed completely after a job loss or some other major life stressor. Chronic stress is a whole-body emotional experience that touches on every aspect of life.

Why Manage Stress?

You know intuitively that it's bad for you when you're pushed too hard, either by yourself or by the world you live in. You also know that it's uncomfortable to have that feeling of stress from day to day. It takes away from your enjoyment of life and diminishes the sense of peace in your heart that is your birthright. But stress isn't just uncomfortable; it's dangerous to your health. Evidence is mounting to support the strong link between chronic stress and a variety of health problems. Upper respiratory infections, coronary artery disease, autoimmune disorders, poor wound healing, depression: all of these problems and many others are made worse by chronic stress.

Robert M. Sapolsky, author of *Why Zebras Don't Get Ulcers* (2004), is one of our nation's leading experts on the physiology of stress. He and others have presented solid evidence that stress affects most of the basic functions of living, including sleep, memory, managing pain, sexual activity, and getting nourishment from food. The effects of stress on aging are another hot topic. It's becoming well known that many of the changes usually attributed to "just getting old" are actually caused or accelerated by stress. These changes include the graying of your hair, the decline of your immune system, the aches and pains you accumulate, and your basic ability to learn new information and remember all the wonderful things that have happened to you along the way.

How does stress exert its harmful effects on the body and mind? There are several major pathways between stress and health, including wear and tear on the body, changes in the function of the immune system, and changes in behavior.

STRESS CAUSES WEAR AND TEAR

Consider the physical changes that happen when a threat appears. Heart rate and blood pressure increase, muscle tension increases, and digestion becomes disrupted. Over time, these conditions cause excessive wear and tear on the organs involved. The heart has to work harder to keep its rate up and push against elevated blood pressure. Muscles get tired, sore, and crampy from chronic tension. Lower back pain is a hallmark of chronic stress. And if digestion is frequently disrupted by stress, food can't be digested and absorbed properly. This deprives the body of the nutrients it needs to thrive.

There is now evidence that chronic stress directly affects how your cells age (Epel et al. 2004). Every cell in your body has a programmed time to die, when the chromosomes will cease to function and the cell won't be able to carry out its normal activities any more. The schedule varies from one cell type to another, but the basic process is the same. Scientists can measure the age of a cell by examining its chromosomes. Recent research shows a clear relationship between perceived stress and premature aging and death of cells in the immune system.

Another way that stress causes wear and tear is by interfering with the restorative process of sleep. Sleep is vitally important for mental and physical health. It's a time when all the body's cells can rest and restore themselves and repair the damage wrought by the stresses and challenges of the day. If you're having problems sleeping, stress is probably a factor in your insomnia. Learning and practicing stress management skills can promote better sleep.

STRESS INCREASES YOUR RISK FOR DISEASE, EARLY DEATH, AND DEPRESSION

Stress has well-known effects on the cardiovascular system. People who are chronically stressed tend to have higher blood pressure, more frequent heart attacks, and a higher incidence of arrhythmias that can be fatal (Schwartz et al. 2003). Cortisol is produced by the body in response to stress. High cortisol levels are related to elevated blood triglycerides and increases in blood levels of insulin and glucose. These three changes are part of *metabolic syndrome*, a newly understood risk factor for heart disease. Cortisol seems to promote metabolic syndrome, which is also recognized to be a risk factor for obesity.

Stress of all kinds is linked to dying prematurely. Some of the pathways linking the two are related to the direct effects of stress on the nervous system and the heart. The stress of beginning a new week or a new month leads to an increase in deaths from heart attacks (Maynard 2000).

The links between chronic stress and depression are strong. Charles Holahan and his colleagues published a review of the evidence for these links in 2005. The picture that emerges is distressing. Stress and depression are linked in a positive feedback loop in which being depressed leads to behaviors that generate stress (for example, by interfering with your relationships), which in turn causes more depression. A hallmark of depression is the use of *avoidant* coping strategies such as denial, social isolation, and minimizing the importance of events. Avoidant coping, as you'll see in chapter 2, is associated with stress, depression, and poorer health. It can be changed, however, and you'll learn better, more active coping techniques.

STRESS HARMS YOUR IMMUNITY

The effects of stress on the immune system have caught huge amounts of attention and research funding over the last decade. One of the most prominent researchers in the field, Janice Kiecolt-Glaser, has published hundreds of articles describing the links between stress, immune function, and disease. She has studied these links in all types of people, from unhappily married women to medical students to elderly people caring for spouses with Alzheimer's disease. In all of this research, a common theme has emerged: stress hormones have a direct influence on immune cells. In the short term, as explained by Robert Sapolsky (2004), stress hormones actually enhance immunity. But this effect quickly fades, and the long-term effects are disruptive and, in some cases, harmful.

You need strong, tightly controlled immune function to sort out intruders from healthy body tissue. Intruders must be quickly controlled, killed, and eliminated from the body. Stress disrupts this process in a variety of ways, resulting in problems like autoimmune disease, increased vulnerability to infection, and slow wound healing. Some of the latest research in this area involves the effects of a stress hormone produced in the brain called *neuropeptide Y*, which appears to cause immune suppression when released in abundance. Neuropeptide Y is involved in emotions and depression, and it appears to be an important link between mood, stress, and immunity (Southwick et al. 1999).

A hot topic in medicine today is the newly understood role of inflammation in cardiovascular diseases. *Arterial plaque*, the buildup of fatty deposits in the arteries that can cause heart attacks and strokes, was once considered a by-product of blood cholesterol. There is now considerable evidence that the development of arterial plaque is helped along by inflammation (Glaser 2005). Inflammation is low-level, chronic over-activity of the immune system. Stress works on the immune system to create more inflammation in the body. This is a big piece of the puzzle linking stress to change in immune function to changes in arterial plaque and, ultimately, to heart disease.

STRESS INFLUENCES YOUR HEALTH HABITS

You probably already have a basic idea of what you need to do to stay healthy: exercise regularly, don't smoke, eat a whole foods–based diet, consume alcohol in moderation, and so on. All of these things have direct effects on the health of your body, mind, and spirit. Yet perhaps you, like so many people, just don't maintain a healthy lifestyle. Why? It's not because you don't care about yourself. It's probably because of stress.

When you feel stress, you want to do something about it, because it's uncomfortable. Stressful feelings often arise during busy times, when there's just too much to do. In the midst of a hassle-ridden day, the quickest fix is often the one people reach for. Smoking a cigarette is one example. Stress and smoking go together; it's a popular stress management tool. It feels like a break, and many people say it's soothing. However, the soothing effect of each cigarette is actually the easing of the tension of nicotine withdrawal. Being a smoker adds the stress of being addicted to your life. Every smoker is on a schedule of stress ⇒ relief ⇒ stress ⇒ relief. That in itself is harmful, along with all the effects smoking has on the heart, lungs, skin, and every other organ of the body.

Debbie Ng and Robert Jeffery (2003) of the University of Minnesota found that, in addition to smoking more, people who feel that they're under high levels of stress exercise less and eat more fatty foods. Ng and Jeffery suggest that stress triggers unhealthy behaviors as an attempt to manage the bad mood that goes along with it. The simple truth is that many people take great pleasure in fatty foods and sedentary behavior. It takes persistence and motivation to eat healthily and exercise regularly long enough to reap the benefits in mood and health. In the meantime, many time-crunched, stressed-out people only feel more pressure trying to adopt these behaviors, and they give up. If unhealthy behaviors are a problem for you, try some of the stress management solutions in this book before you start to make big changes in your health habits.

New Discoveries About Stress

There is a constant flow of new research on stress, its effects, and how to manage it effectively. In recent years, we've learned astounding things about how stress affects immunity, aging, and communities. We're starting to understand what it is about our modern age that is so stressful and what we can do about it, as individuals and as a society.

An entire new field of science, *psychoneuroimmunology* (the study of how thoughts and emotions are linked to health through the immune, nervous, endocrine, and other body systems), has blossomed in the last fifteen years. The pioneers of this field are passionate about learning and teaching us about the connections between stress, immunity, disease, mood, and perception. This is a particularly vibrant area because new discoveries can be applied quickly and directly to improve people's daily lives.

Yes, evidence of the harmful effects of stress is mounting, but that's only half of the story. Innovative approaches like self-expression, emotional intelligence, and skillful interpersonal communication are emerging to help people manage stress. We've gained new insight into *flow*, a focused, relaxed, productive state of consciousness that anyone can learn to access. New technologies like at-home biofeedback training, full-spectrum lights, and specially engineered music are helping create internal and external environments that reduce stress. We know more about how tried-and-true remedies like exercise and meditation work to counteract stress.

On a larger scale, we're seeing noise-reduction laws in cities, more flexible work schedules, specially designed hospital rooms—all evidence that on every level, we're looking for ways to make life less stressful, because stress reduction has become something we value as individuals and as a society. We're learning how to make stress management work for people of all ages in all sorts of environments. Stress management is no longer a luxury for people who have all of their basic needs met. Stress management is a basic need, and we're beginning to know how best to use it.

Mind-Body Medicine: A New Approach to Being Well

Most of the solutions you'll learn in this book come from the field of mind-body medicine (MBM). They've been used successfully with thousands of people all over the world to deal with all types of stress. The Center for Mind-Body Medicine in Washington, DC, conducts group workshops for people who want to learn better stress management and self-care. The center also offers training to health professionals in the United States, the Middle East, and Kosovo, helping them work more compassionately and effectively with their clients.

HOW IS MBM DIFFERENT?

MBM is a relatively new field that brings together researchers and clinicians from the fields of biomedicine, health psychology, public health, nursing, and psychotherapy. MBM is guided by the premise that mind, body, and spirit are integral parts of a system. Information flows to and from these aspects of a person all the time, and they can't be separated. A stressor that affects the mind also affects the body and spirit. Doing something that helps heal your spirit will also heal your body and mind.

From this perspective, all types of illness take on new meaning. Mental illness can be seen as a spiritual crisis as well as a physical condition that can be helped with diet, exercise, and other body-focused treatments. In *The Mindbody Prescription: Healing the Body, Healing the Pain* (1998), John Sarno explains the fascinating connections between lower back and other musculoskeletal pain and emotional well-being. His prescription includes emotional as well as body work. MBM has provided us with creative and effective ways to manage the nagging ailments related to chronic stress.

MBM Is Holistic

MBM recognizes the person as a system of relationships between body, mind, and spirit. It recognizes the interconnections among people, and between people and the environment. Connections between people and the divine (however you think of it) are recognized as important issues in staying well or coping with illness. Social support is a well-known buffer between stress and the mind-body systems. It's so important to have good, kind connections with other people, and isolation and loneliness are important risk factors for a variety of illnesses. Finally, MBM seeks to empower people to take control of their own health.

MBM Emphasizes Strengths, Not Pathology

MBM is not pathology-based like traditional medicine and psychology. You are not labeled with a diagnosis and prescribed a treatment that you're expected to "comply" with. This model of healing has its role in some situations, but for most people, it's demeaning and often ineffective. MBM trusts each person to have ideas about what's going on and what will help. The best expert on your health is you.

By shifting the focus from problems and pathology, MBM brings strengths and resources to the fore. A person with a new diagnosis might have a strong social network and a good marriage. Making these resources part of the treatment plan is vital to helping the whole person cope with the challenge of illness.

It's easy to lose sight of what's going well for you when you feel overwhelmed by what's creating difficulty.

Optimism and pessimism have profound health effects. In chapter 3, you'll learn more about positive psychology and take a good look at what you have going for you in your life and how you can use your many strengths and talents to take better care of yourself.

HOW MBM CAN HELP YOU CHANGE

MBM relies on you to take the initiative in improving your health. In this book, you won't be asked to do as you're told. On the contrary, you'll be asked what you've been doing and what you can do from now on to make your own life better. You'll be given new insight, information, support, and skills to make deep, lasting changes in your life. They might be very obvious changes, like overhauling your diet or starting a daily meditation practice. The changes might also be subtle, like being a little slower to get angry in traffic, more attentive when someone speaks to you, or more likely to notice a beautiful flower as you walk to your car on your way to work in the morning. All of these changes come from seeing yourself and your life with fresh eyes. They come from your understanding of where stress comes from and how it affects you, and from knowing you have the tools to minimize the bad effects of stress and embrace what it can offer you in the form of a sense of excitement and accomplishment.

Reaching the Body Through the Mind

Many of the techniques of MBM work by changing thought patterns and emotional states from anxious to calm. This simple shift causes big changes in your body. Your heart rate slows, breathing deepens, muscles relax, and blood flow to your digestive organs increases. Your body gets a break from the constant pressure of stress. Over time, as you practice these techniques, it becomes easier and easier to shift from overdrive to neutral. Thinking becomes clearer, your body feels better, and life seems more manageable.

Some MBM techniques—notably guided imagery, disclosure, and hypnosis—have been shown to have real, reliable effects on the immune system (Miller and Cohen 2001). This is a very active area of research, and new information is published every month about how thoughts and emotions can affect immunity. It's becoming clear that stress management skills are important to good immune function and disease prevention. We'll explore these skills and more in chapters 4, 7, and 9.

Self-Awareness and Self-Regulation

MBM begins with learning to pay closer attention to how you're doing. In this book, you'll discover ways to recognize stress in your body and mind before it starts to hurt you. Self-awareness is a part of all ten simple solutions. You can't make an intelligent change if you aren't clear about what you're changing.

Do you have old beliefs and fears that are making it hard for you to relax and be happy? We'll address your thoughts and how they can help and hurt you in chapter 4. Do you get home from work and realize your shoulders have been hunched all day and now they're stiff and sore, making you want to collapse in a chair instead of taking a walk outside? In chapter 6, you'll learn what your body cues to stress are and how to prevent stress from taking up permanent residence in your muscles and joints. Perhaps you tend to argue with your spouse about seemingly trivial things. It starts as a conversation, and before you know it, you're both irritated and tense. In chapter 8, you'll learn to recognize your conversational triggers for stress. You'll learn techniques for listening both to yourself and to your partner during important conversations.

Before you dive in to the ten simple solutions, complete these two exercises. The first will help you clarify where you are now and where you'd like to go. The second will help you commit to getting there. For these exercises and others in the book, you may want to use a notebook dedicated to your stress management program.

Exercise: Self-Assessment for Readiness to Change

Here's an exercise that will give you a different view of yourself and your goals. It involves drawing, but you're certainly not expected to create a photographic likeness of anyone or anything. The images you create will come from a place inside you that doesn't use words to express itself, but is in closer touch with your intuition and inner wisdom.

Before you start, gather some materials. You'll need your notebook. You'll also need three sheets of plain white paper. Find some pencils, crayons, or markers in a variety of colors. If you don't have any, consider buying a small box of colored pencils. You can use them in your journal and for drawings in other exercises in this book.

Now, with your materials gathered, sit in a comfortable spot, at a table or on the floor, as long as you have a firm surface to support your paper. You're going to create three images. Read these instructions, do the mental imagery, and then draw. Don't stop to think about what you're drawing. Just move the marker over the paper and allow what wants to emerge to come through. Trust yourself.

IMAGE ONE. Close your eyes and scan your body for muscle tension. Take a moment to think about that tension melting away. Think about letting go and making yourself soft and receptive. When you feel a shift, settle into it and ask yourself a question:

How am I doing?

Allow whatever images come to mind to flow past. Just ask the question and sit with it for a minute or so. Don't latch on to any one idea; just let them flow.

Now, pick up whatever marker appeals to you and start to draw. Use whatever colors you're attracted to. Just create an image that reflects the answer to the question *How am I doing?*

Continue for a minute or two, no longer. This is meant to be a quick, intuitive exercise.

IMAGE TWO. Repeat the calming and centering step you did before making the first image. This time, ask yourself this question:

What bothers me?

Again, take a minute or two to create an image that addresses this question.

IMAGE THREE. Repeat the calming and centering moment. Now ask yourself this question:

What makes me happy now?

Take a minute or two to create an image that addresses this question.

Now, take all three drawings and lay them in front of you in the order you drew them. You're going to analyze each image. Record your responses in your journal.

Start by looking at your first drawing and answering these questions. Then do the same for the next two pictures.

1. What's the overall tone of the image? What word does it bring up for you when you look at it?

2. What are the prominent features of the image? Are there objects, people, colors, or shapes that catch your eye? Write down what they are.

3. Now look for more subtle aspects of the drawing. Is there a little squiggle somewhere that means something to you? Write about it.

Now, look at the three images as a group and consider these questions: Are there things they have in common? Did you use similar colors? Do some have more energy than others? How do they seem to fit together? Write about that.

You'll use these images and what you've written about them as indications of the stressors in your life and the resources you have to deal with them. You're about to embark on a process of personal growth, and it's good to have some clarity about where you are and where you're going.

Now, on a fresh page, make three columns. Label the first column "Me: Now." Looking at the first image you drew, make a list of five to ten adjectives and short phrases that describe you, now.

In the second column, make a list of stressors. Let your second image and the writing you did about it be your guide. Some of the items on the list may be obvious, but chances are that some things you hadn't previously considered stressors will appear on your list.

In the third column, list resources. Start by looking at the third image and your written analysis of it. Now generate a simple list of the good things in your life. These will be things about you: things about your home, relationships, and work—whatever it is in your life that enriches you. These are the tools you'll be using in chapters 2 and 3 when you explore healthy coping and living from a place of strength and confidence.

Now take a few moments to reflect on the exercise, and write whatever comes to you in your journal. This is information that you will turn to several times as you learn the solutions in this book, and perhaps long after you've finished. I recommend doing this exercise every couple of months while you're making changes in your life, and then at least once or twice a year afterward. The more loving, well-intentioned attention you give yourself, the more consciously and mindfully you'll live.

Exercise: Write a Contract

Now it's time to make a commitment to managing stress. You've learned what it is and what it can do to your health. You've learned that there are very effective ways to prevent it from causing problems in your life. I hope that by now, you're excited about becoming adept at managing stress and living a calmer, healthier life.

You are more likely to be able to make a change in your life if you make a written commitment to do so. There's something almost magical about writing something down and signing your name to it. It's a document you can return to when your motivation is flagging. It's an intention to take better care of yourself. If and when you falter, there's no reason to beat yourself up about it. You're doing the best you can. Just remind yourself of your intention and start over. Every good thing you do counts.

Open your journal to a blank page. At the top, write the date. Then write a short, succinct paragraph stating your intentions about overcoming the stress in your life. Here's an example:

> *I, Claire Wheeler, resolve that I will take as much time as necessary to learn at least one of the simple solutions to stress in this book. I will start today by reading the chapter and doing the recommended exercises. I will learn more about myself and how stress affects me, and I'll make time in my daily schedule to practice the skill that I choose to learn.*

After your paragraph, sign your name.

That's it. Mark the page somehow so it's easy to find whenever you want to read your contract. If you want to add to it or change it, you can, or you can start over with a new intention. This technique works well for all kinds of behavior changes.

Conclusion

We've covered a lot of ground in this introduction. You've looked at all the ways stress can affect your health in body, mind, and spirit. You've learned that stress works in many ways to hurt you, but you have some control over the situation. Most importantly, you've learned that stress is a real threat to your health and well-being, and stress management is not a luxury but a basic necessity in our modern, fast-paced world.

1

Assess Your
Level of Stress

Here's some good news: by simply reading and learning about stress, you may already be countering its effects on your life. People who enter a stress management program show improvement in their stress levels after the first informational session—before learning any new skills or strategies. But you're only getting started in the process of managing stress.

In this chapter, you'll take a close look at how you're doing now managing the stressors you face in your everyday life. We'll investigate the ways—some obvious, some subtle—that stress may be affecting you.

Self-Assessment for Stress Risk

What is your risk for having a problem with stress now? There are many tools for answering this question. In 1967, Thomas Holmes and Richard Rahe proposed that taking an inventory of major life events could predict whether a person's health would be affected by stress. The thinking was that any life change, whether positive or negative, creates stress, in part because all changes involve loss, changes in habits, and a shift in responsibilities. Major life events such as a job change, marriage, or divorce also frequently include a change of identity, social status, interpersonal connections, and other basic life circumstances.

Taking stock of the major events in your life is a good starting point for thinking about the stresses you've encountered. However, since 1967 we've learned that while major life events may predict later stress-related illnesses for some people, there are other factors that are equally if not more important. Research shows that the stress of daily hassles can be more harmful to health than the stress of the big events (Fuller et al. 2003; Larson, Ader, and Moynihan 2001). These hassles are often part of working life, but they can come from any source: neighbors, traffic, noise, even an oppressive social environment.

For this next exercise, though, we'll focus on major life events.

Exercise: Assess Your Life for Stressful Events and Their Effects

The first part of this exercise is a simple review of the past year and the past month of your life, focusing on any important changes and challenges you've had to cope with. You'll notice that some of these events may be framed as positive, some as negative, and some as neutral. Most of the items on the list have been recognized in research as potential causes of stress.

Take a look at the list, and check off the events that have happened to you in the last year. Then go over it again, making another set of checks for the past month.

Life Event	Last Year	Last Month
Relationship Events		
death of your spouse or significant other (S/O)	☐	☐
Serious injury or illness in your spouse or S/O	☐	☐
Serious injury or illness in your child	☐	☐
Divorce or separation from your S/O	☐	☐
Death of a close family member	☐	☐
Beginning cohabitation with your S/O	☐	☐
Marriage	☐	☐
New pregnancy	☐	☐
Birth or adoption of a child	☐	☐
Children leaving home	☐	☐
Other	☐	☐
Other	☐	☐
Work/Financial Events		
Job loss	☐	☐
Retirement	☐	☐
Job transfer	☐	☐
New job	☐	☐
Starting school	☐	☐
Graduation	☐	☐
Significant conflict at work	☐	☐
Losing an advancement/ promotion at work	☐	☐

Life Event	Past Year	Past Month
Financial setback (investments, pension plan, etc.)	☐	☐
Financial windfall (inheritance, etc.)	☐	☐
Other	☐	☐
Other	☐	☐
Health Events		
Newly diagnosed illness	☐	☐
Serious injury	☐	☐
Surgery	☐	☐
New aches or pains	☐	☐
Other	☐	☐
Other	☐	☐
Other Events		
Moving	☐	☐
Major vacation	☐	☐
Large purchase (car, RV, boat, etc.)	☐	☐
Dieting or beginning exercise program	☐	☐
Other	☐	☐
Other	☐	☐

Now count up the number of challenges you've encountered in the past year and in the past month. It's helpful to look at your score in each category as well as your total score. You may find that your life has been very stable in the areas of work and finance, but turbulent in your relationships or other areas. Noticing this will help you appreciate the stability that you do have in your life while coping with the changes that you're experiencing. In general, the higher your score overall, the more likely it is that you've been challenged to cope in healthy, constructive ways—or tempted to manage stress with behaviors that aren't good for you in the long run.

This exercise can give you some perspective on the number of stressful life events you've experienced, but it tells only part of the story. The biggest limitation to this approach is that stress is subjective. Each item on the list will have a completely different meaning to—and effect on—each person who experiences it.

Now, look at your results with a different twist. From the list, choose the event that had the most significant impact on your life. Take some time to reflect on this event, and ask yourself the following questions. Write your answers in your journal.

1. How was my health just before this happened?

2. What was my general mood and state of mind before it happened?

3. In the two to four weeks after this event, did I develop a cold or other health problem?

4. In the two to four weeks after this event, did I develop any new aches or pains?

5. Did my sleep habits change during and after this challenge?

6. Did I have anyone to turn to for emotional support when this was happening?

7. Did my use of alcohol, cigarettes, other drugs, TV, or the computer increase during this situation?

8. How long did it take for me to start to feel normal after this happened?

9. Was I able to find anything positive about the experience? Did I learn anything from it that will help me in the future?

Answering these questions will give you solid, useful information about your susceptibility to the effects of stress, and your coping style. In the next chapter, I'll go into great detail about coping styles, but for now it's important for you to recognize and acknowledge how change and loss affect you. If you like, go back and answer questions 1 through 9 about another significant event on your list.

DOES STRESS AFFECT YOUR PHYSICAL HEALTH?

Did you answer yes to question 3 (a cold or other health problem) or question 4 (new aches or pains)? If so, you may have a close link between life stresses and your immune strength. You may be carrying a load of chronic stress in your body and mind that make you especially vulnerable to the health effects of stress. If you developed a cold or other illness, your immune system is probably most affected. If you developed aches or pains, both your immune system and your overall state of tension may be a problem. Working with some of the techniques in this book can help you get better control over your responses to stressful events and add to your resilience.

DOES STRESS ROB YOU OF A GOOD NIGHT'S SLEEP?

Insomnia, or difficulty falling asleep or staying asleep, is an almost universal response to acute stressors and big challenges. Stressful events often lead to (and are made worse by) anxious thinking. This is often a result of making dire appraisals about the event and all its possible outcomes. Do you tend to catastrophize bad events, automatically going to the worst possible outcome of a situation? Do you blow things out of proportion, only to have them blow over? Do you find yourself ruminating without coming to any useful conclusions or plans? It may be helpful for you to read chapter 4. Learning to manage anxious thinking will help you ride through storms with a calmer, clearer mind and get a better night's sleep.

Sometimes, stress-related insomnia is more a matter of physical restlessness and arousal than nonstop thinking. During a stressful time, your sympathetic nervous system is activated more than usual. You have more adrenaline flowing in your veins day and night.

There are some extremely effective ways to manage this. The first is physical exercise. This would preferably be strenuous, aerobic exercise, for thirty to fifty minutes each day. If that's not something you can do now, simple stretching, dancing, or yoga can make a big difference. We'll look at a body-based approach to managing stress in chapter 6.

If insomnia is a matter of simply not being able to relax your body, you can learn ways to do that as well. In chapters 6 and 9, we'll look at specific practices you can use to relax your body and mind. Try a few of them, and choose one to do every day for a few weeks. You'll find a variety of exercises in this book for relaxation, and one of them is bound to appeal to you.

HOW'S YOUR SOCIAL SUPPORT?

If you answered no to question 6 (someone to turn to for emotional support), you may need to think about developing a social support system. This sounds daunting, but it doesn't have to be. What you can do is take stock of the relationships you already have in your life and think about how you can make them more mutually supportive.

This often requires learning new skills, which we'll explore in chapter 8. Being able to connect with other people, from the grocery store checker to your spouse, with more patience and humanity will not only protect you from the ravages of stress, it will also make other people happier. There are many ways that relationships can add stress to your life, but these usually involve difficulty setting good boundaries, saying no to demands, and asking for what you want (without whining). Strong, healthy relationships improve your resilience.

DOES STRESS CHANGE YOUR USE OF SUBSTANCES?

Question 7 asks about your use of substances during times of stress. For many people, alcohol or fatty food used in moderation is an enjoyable part of life. During stressful periods, however, people tend to use these more, looking for a quick jolt of pleasure that will take them away from the challenges of the present moment. However, it's not just pleasure that people are seeking. They may be using substances to try to counteract the symptoms of stress—for example, using caffeine during the day to stay awake and productive when they're not getting enough sleep, or using sleeping pills when they're having difficulty falling asleep. In chapter 5, you'll see that stress actually changes your appetite, shifting your preferences away from healthy food and toward fatty, sweet foods that calm your brain chemistry.

The dangers in this approach to stress management are many. Most of the substances used for avoidant coping tend to be addictive. Once the crisis is over, it's hard to let go of a newly acquired smoking habit, for example. And when you add the effects of a strong, short-term stressor to the effects of bad diet and too much alcohol, the body and mind suffer more than they should. This creates even more opportunity for aging, illness, and psychological distress to take hold.

In chapter 2, I'll explain the difference between avoidant and active coping, and you'll learn how to shift from one to the other. In chapter 5, you'll learn how to use food as a type of medicine. You can eat comfort foods without harming yourself if you choose healthy foods and find comfort in the actual preparation of food—and the joy of savoring a good meal instead of bolting something down for a momentary sugar fix.

CAN YOU RISE ABOVE IT?

Questions 8 and 9 address your resiliency. How long does it take you to recover from a stressful incident? Can you survive a stressful event and feel that, even though you didn't ask for it and wouldn't choose to experience it again, you still got something positive out of it? When you're in the thick of a crisis, finding or creating some kind of positive meaning gives you strength to see things through. In chapter 10, we'll explore ways to bring a sense of transcendence and inner peace to each day's challenges.

How Is Stress Affecting You Now?

In the following exercise, we're going to look at sets of symptoms that are associated with the effects of ongoing stress on the body, mind, and relationships. This will help you determine whether—and how—you're suffering from chronic stress.

Exercise: Evaluate Your Stress Symptoms

For each list, rate how often you experience each symptom. Use the following scale:

never	1
seldom	2
often	3
daily	4

Then total your score for each symptom list.

Physical Symptoms

indigestion	_____
shoulder tension	_____
headaches	_____
jaw clenching	_____
racing heartbeat	_____
changes in appetite	_____
cold, sweaty palms	_____
constipation or diarrhea	_____
Total:	_____

Psychological/Emotional Symptoms

difficulty concentrating	_____
insomnia	_____
feeling nervous	_____
increased alcohol use	_____
feeling rushed	_____
feeling sad or hopeless	_____
forgetting important things	_____
increased use of TV or computer	_____
Total:	_____

Social Symptoms

decreased interest in sex	_____
frequent arguments with partner	_____
feelings of hostility	_____
impatience with others	_____
lack of interest in socializing	_____
avoiding friends	_____
feeling jealousy	_____
withholding affection	_____
Total:	_____

For each group of symptoms, use the following score ranges as a general guide:

8–14. Stress is creating few problems for you in this area. That doesn't mean you don't perceive stress or need to learn to manage it. You may simply be in a relatively stable, comfortable time in your life. Use your results from the first exercise in this chapter to guide you to solutions that will help maintain your current low-stress state.

15–19. Stress is starting to show up in your body, mind, or relationships. It might not be serious now, but it will be helpful to learn some solutions to stress so you can get these symptoms, in their early stages, under control. This will help you avoid the health consequences of stress over time, and add to your enjoyment of life.

20–25. Stress is becoming a problem for you. If you scored any group of symptoms in this range, you could be at risk for illness or relationship problems. Now is the time to start managing your stress. If you feel overwhelmed by the thought of doing this on your own, you might benefit from a visit to your primary care physician for a referral. It's time to start taking better care of yourself.

26–32. You are likely very aware that stress is a problem for you. You may be having health problems already. It's important that you make a new commitment to caring for your health and your relationships. A visit to your physician for a physical exam may be in order.

Conclusion

In this chapter, you learned how you are affected by stressful life events. You also examined the possible effects that stress may be having on your life now. Using the information you gathered here, you can make a good decision about what to do next. What area of stress management do you want to focus on first? Remember, body, mind, and spirit are intimately entwined. Wherever you start, you'll be taking the first step toward less stress and better health in all parts of you and your life.

Find a Healthy Way to Cope

Coping and stress go hand in hand. Coping is anything you do to relieve any unsettling effects of stressful events in your life. When you think of it that way, you'll realize that you are coping all day long, frequently without your being aware of it. All types of stress, from traffic snarls to arguments with your partner, call upon coping responses, and it's up to you to learn and use coping strategies that serve your overall well-being for the long term.

Many of the things we think of as bad habits are actually misguided coping strategies, those that only lead to more problems and more stress. These unhelpful coping responses include watching too much television, drinking alcohol, procrastinating, and eating comfort foods.

In this chapter, we'll look at how stress relates to coping and how you can cope better by coping consciously. You'll gain insight into your own coping style and learn new responses and resources for dealing with stress.

How Do You Cope Now?

The following exercise is an abbreviated version of the brief COPE questionnaire, developed by Charles Carver (1997) with

Michael Scheier and Jagdish Weintraub for research on coping styles. You can use this questionnaire to get a quick read on some of the coping strategies you tend to use.

Exercise: COPE Questionnaire

Rate how often you use each of the following possible ways of dealing with stressful events in your life. Use the following scale:

I don't do this at all	1
I do this a little bit	2
I do this in moderation	3
I do this a lot	4

It may be that you use different approaches for different types of stress. Try to answer based on how you generally respond to most of the stresses you face each day.

1. I turn to work and other activities to take my mind off things   _____

2. I concentrate my efforts on doing something about the situation that's bothering me   _____

3. I say to myself, "This isn't real"   _____

4. I use alcohol or drugs to make myself feel better   _____

5. I get emotional support from others   _____

6. I take action to try to make the situation better   _____

7. I refuse to believe that it has happened   _____

8. I say things to let my unpleasant feelings escape _____

9. I get help and advice from other people _____

10. I use alcohol or other drugs to help me get through it _____

11. I try to see it in a different light, to make it seem more positive _____

12. I try to come up with a strategy about what to do _____

13. I get comfort and understanding from someone _____

14. I look for something good in what's happening _____

15. I do something to think about it less, like going to movies, watching TV, reading, daydreaming, sleeping, or shopping _____

16. I accept the reality of the fact that it has happened _____

17. I express my negative feelings _____

18. I try to find comfort in my religious or spiritual beliefs _____

19. I try to get advice or help from other people about what to do _____

20. I try to learn to live with it _____

21. I think hard about what steps to take _____

22. I pray or meditate _____

Now calculate your scores for each coping strategy and record them in your stress notebook.

Items	Coping Strategy
1 and 15	self-distraction
2 and 6	active coping
3 and 7	denial
4 and 10	substance use
5 and 13	use of emotional social support
9 and 19	use of instrumental social support
8 and 17	venting
11 and 14	positive reframing
12 and 21	planning
16 and 20	acceptance
18 and 22	transcendence

Keep these scores handy as you read this chapter, because we'll look at each of these strategies to see how they can help or hinder your coping. If you use methods that aren't helpful, you can learn to use coping skills that will better serve you as you face stress in your life.

Understanding Coping as a Two-Step Process

Much has been written about coping in the health and psychology literature because it's such an important part of staying well and being happy. Coping is a two-stage process of appraisal—that is, making judgments about what's happening and what you're going to do about it (Folkman et al. 1986). The first step is *primary appraisal*, in which you decide whether something is a threat to you or your interests. The *secondary appraisal* concerns whether there's anything you can do to change the situation to minimize bad outcomes and increase the possibility of positive outcomes. Based on primary and secondary appraisals, you make decisions (whether consciously or unconsciously) about how you're going to respond to the stressor—in other words, you decide what coping strategies you will use. This entire process is influenced by your personality, experience, beliefs, and other fundamental qualities that make you an individual. If you're interested in exploring those aspects of coping, you can do so in chapter 3.

PRIMARY APPRAISALS

In the primary appraisal, you determine what's at stake in the situation. This applies to any kind of stressor, from a traffic jam to a medical diagnosis or a fight with your spouse. In a traffic jam, what's at stake may be being late to work, being hassled by your boss, or feeling guilty. As the stressors become more serious, as in the case of a medical diagnosis, the stakes get higher and the potential for distress increases. Minor stresses, however, can inflict a lot of psychological and emotional damage if there are lots of them happening every day. Your primary appraisal of minor stressors can become more dire if you start to see them as inevitable or uncontrollable.

Primary appraisals can run the gamut from total denial of the significance of the event to overt catastrophizing. Finding a middle ground and being as realistic as possible about the potential outcomes of a stressful situation can go a long way toward averting an excessive stress reaction in body and mind. Primary appraisals are important because they set the stage for your responses. It's helpful to become aware of your appraisals because they may be inaccurate or based on assumptions and old thought processes that aren't useful or relevant in your life.

Exercise: Track Your Primary Appraisals

For this exercise, you'll need to carry your stress management notebook with you for an entire day. Ideally, this would be a typical day in which you take care of your usual responsibilities. Begin the day by setting the intention to be aware of everything that bothers you for the entire day and to write it down in your notebook. Set this intention before you get out of bed—in fact, it's best to have the notebook on your nightstand so you can start recording as soon as something comes up. You may discover that the parade of stressors begins in your mind as soon as you wake up in the morning, before your feet even hit the floor. If so, just go with it, and make a list of your worries or concerns on a blank page.

Continue listing stressors as they arise throughout the day. Remember, these can be things that are actually happening, or simply thoughts that cause you to feel uncomfortable, worried, or anxious. These are all potential stressors. It may surprise you to see how many of them you encounter in an average day.

Here's an example of what your entries may look like:

6:30 A.M. *It's raining, and traffic is going to be slow*

6:32 A.M. *I have a big presentation to make today, and I feel unprepared*

6:45 A.M. *I feel fat and I don't have anything I like to wear*

7:30 A.M. *I was right, the traffic is really bad this morning*

9:25 A.M. *My computer has lost my presentation file! Disaster!*

10:40 A.M. *I found the file, but I was so frazzled I blew the presentation*

1:00 P.M. *I wanted to have lunch with my husband, but he couldn't make it*

1:05 P.M. *He's always too busy to eat lunch with me ...*

3:30 P.M. *My boss told me my presentation seemed choppy and disorganized*

5:00 P.M. *Heavy traffic on the way home, and I still need to grocery shop*

6:30 P.M. *Had an argument with my husband about missing lunch with me*

8:00 P.M. *Looking over the mail—the gas bill is twice what I expected*

Now, find some time as soon as possible after your observation day to sit down with your list. For each item on the list, ask two questions:

1. What is at stake here? What can I lose or how can this harm me?

2. How likely is it that something bad will happen as a result of this event?

Chances are that for many of the potential stressors you encounter each day, the actual threat to your well-being is not as great as it may have felt at the time. With practice, you will learn to ask these two questions in the moment, as the stress is occurring. This way, you can stop automatic stress responses before they happen.

You can make *acceptance coping* part of your primary appraisal. Acceptance coping is simply acknowledging the reality of the challenges you're facing. You might tell yourself, *I'm learning to deal with it* and *I've come to terms with the fact that this is happening*. Once you do this, you can move on to the next stage of coping, which is figuring out how much, if any, control you have over the outcome. From there, you can decide what you're going to do about it. All of this starts with a sense of acceptance that is not the same as being resigned *(This is happening and there's nothing I can do about it)*. There is always *something* you can do when life presents you with a challenge, but first you have to accept the fact that it's happening at all.

In a study of college students with varying levels of life stress, Victoria Burns and her colleagues (2002) found that those who tended to use acceptance coping were able to mount a more effective immune response to a flu shot than those who didn't use acceptance coping. Apparently there is something stressful about denial and suppression that we can't really identify, but its effects are real and measurable.

Working with primary appraisals involves putting the events of daily life into a larger perspective. It's also helpful to explore the roots of your negative appraisals of life's events. There are many reasons that relatively minor, harmless events can trigger a sense of threat. Some possibilities include:

- Minor events remind you of bigger stressors and traumas from the past.

- Daily stressors can trigger memories of painful childhood incidents.

- Daily challenges can tap into erroneous beliefs about vulnerability from the past.

- Stressful events can sometimes be seen as part of a bigger pattern of loss, helplessness, or persecution that doesn't exist.

Going through your list again, ask yourself if any of these—or any other unhelpful assumptions—are affecting how you look at things. If you find that you tend to overestimate the possible negative impact of relatively minor life events, it can be helpful to create a verbal cue that you can say to yourself whenever these things come up. Some examples are:

How interesting!
At least it's not (fill in the blank).
This is manageable.
No big deal.

Humor can be very helpful here. This is not to say that you should minimize the importance of life's stressors to the point that you don't take care of yourself and deal with problems as they arise. The point is to recognize that most of these things, even if they happen repeatedly, are transient and really don't matter much in the big scheme of things. It's a useful skill to be able to recognize catastrophizing when you're doing it, and to gently steer yourself away from always finding the most negative implications of life's difficulties. It's been said that life isn't what happens to you, it's what you think about what happens to you. This idea is very freeing, because it opens up the possibility that you can decide for yourself just how bad or okay the things that happen to you really are.

Another valuable resource when making primary appraisals is the people in your life who are supportive. Talking about what's bothering you can help you reassess the level of threat in the situation, for better or worse. It can provide a reality check to find out whether your perceptions of threat seem realistic to someone you trust.

SECONDARY APPRAISALS

The secondary appraisal involves asking two questions about an event that, in your primary appraisal, you have decided is a threat to you. The first is, *Do I have any control over this situation, and can I change it to make it less threatening?* The second is, *Can I handle the emotions I feel in response to this event and its consequences?* The secondary appraisal can be something that happens in your conscious mind, or it can be an automatic response to your primary appraisal. If you take control over making the secondary appraisal, however, you can be in charge of the coping strategies you use.

You can think of these two questions as the thinking part and the feeling part. The first part, the thinking part, involves assessing your level of control over the situation. This is especially important if you, like many people, feel distress over things you have no control over. The extent to which you can control the situation should determine the strategy you use to deal with it. In a situation that is controllable, it's best to use a direct, active coping approach that will help change things for the better. If the stressor is something you can't control (for example, the weather), it's best to adopt strategies that are more passive and more soothing to your emotional responses.

It's important to be able to tell the difference between situations you can control and those you can't, because a false feeling of control can lead to great emotional distress and interfere with acceptance, something that helps you thrive in the face of stress. This is another way that social support is beneficial. Friends and family can help you figure out whether you have control and what your resources for coping are. They may offer themselves as resources as well, adding to your sense that you can, in fact, cope effectively with the situation.

Using Flexible Coping

Most people have developed coping strategies that they've used for years, and they tend to use them in response to all the stresses they're exposed to. For example, some people tend to become confrontational whenever they feel anxious, scared, or angry. This approach may be helpful in some situations, like dealing with shady salespeople or an incompetent repairman. This approach can be counterproductive, however, when you're stopped for a speeding ticket or you're trying to get a raise. It can also be unhelpful and distressing in relationships.

Other people have a more passive coping style. They rarely seem angry and tend to ignore problems, hoping they'll pass. That can be helpful for stressors that are temporary and minor, like travel delays, traffic jams, and dealing with obnoxious relatives. This type of coping can be a real problem, however, if the stressor is serious and requires action, like filing taxes or taking care of a medical problem.

The most beneficial approach is to be as flexible as possible with your coping strategies, and to learn when to apply what skill from your repertoire. This, according to Robert Sapolsky (2004), is the best use of coping strategies, and coping flexibly is a skill that almost anyone can learn. This is a key concept. You are not a slave to your habitual responses to stress. If you start paying attention to your primary and secondary appraisals, bringing them into the light of day, you will be able to decide what coping style and strategy is going to help you the most. In studies of people trying to quit smoking, coping flexibility was an important factor in keeping them from relapsing (Wenzel, Glanz, and Lerman 2002). Learning to use flexible coping will help you feel more in control, even in situations where you have little control over what's happening. At least you've taken control over your responses, and this is an important way to defuse the power of stress to do harm to your body and mind.

To Cope or Not to Cope?

Before we look at flexible, healthy coping strategies—the ones that really work—let's consider what *doesn't* work.

AVOIDANT COPING

Avoidant coping, or the type that keeps you from confronting an issue and figuring out how to deal with it, is harmful to emotional, psychological, and physical health (Aldwin and Park 2004; Temoshok 1987). This may be due in part to the problems caused by suppressing unwanted emotions and thoughts, as explained by Denise Sloan of Temple University in her 2004 study of avoidance and emotion. According to Sloan, as people exert more effort avoiding what they perceive as negative thoughts and feelings in their daily lives, this disturbing material only becomes more powerful, and leads to psychological symptoms and deterioration in the overall quality of life.

What are avoidant coping strategies? They include denying there's a problem, inappropriately minimizing the importance of a problem, or finding ways to justify inaction in the face of a challenge. There are some occasions when passive, avoidant coping may be more beneficial, or at least more logical. When a stressor is overwhelmingly negative and completely uncontrollable, there are few options except to endure it using avoidant coping methods.

Avoidant coping is not relaxing; quite the contrary. Suppressing thoughts and emotions stimulates the release of stress hormones and raises blood pressure, which causes more wear and tear on the vascular system. Dramatic, overwhelming stressors that call for passive coping aren't part of the typical person's daily life. Habitually using avoidant coping for minor stressors and daily hassles can lead to long-term problems with blood pressure (Hawkley et al. 2005) and depression (Holahan et al. 2005).

Perhaps the most common type of avoidant coping is *distraction*. This is the use of entertainment, food, alcohol, other substances, and even interpersonal drama to avoid confronting problems. This coping method seems to be gaining in popularity as the availability of distraction increases. The Internet, computer games, other electronic games, cell phones, instant messaging, and other media are providing us with twenty-four hours a day of enticing, stimulating distraction from the here and now. These activities have proven to be potentially very addictive, and they have the power to destroy relationships and jeopardize employment. They may seem fun, relaxing, and even harmless in the short run, but for many people, these distracting activities only cause more problems, and more life stress and distress.

Paradoxically, avoidant coping appears to lead to an increase in the number of life stressors a person experiences over time. In their 2005 paper about depression and coping, Charles Holahan and his colleagues speculated that avoidance leads to more problems by way of a lack of effective problem solving. This makes sense; it's the old hiding one's head in the sand cliché made real.

Another form of avoidant coping is *emotional discharge*, which Holahan and his colleagues define as focusing on and expressing negative emotions in the face of a stressor instead of directing attention to confronting the problem that's causing the bad feelings. This can create more problems by alienating the people you rely on for social support and creating drama that only distracts you from the practicalities of the situation at hand. Some problems resolve themselves eventually, but most don't. Ignoring these problems is not an effective way to keep stress at bay, because most will only worsen as a result of your inaction.

PROACTIVE COPING

If avoidant coping doesn't work, what's the alternative? *Proactive coping*, in which you anticipate and take action to prevent stressful situations, may be the best strategy of all. If you can prevent the situation from occurring in the first place, no reactive coping is necessary. Proactive coping, as described by Lisa Aspinwall and Shelley Taylor (1997), is a set of thoughts and actions that are triggered by the recognition that something undesirable might be looming ahead. Aspinwall and Taylor propose that proactive coping takes place in four stages, beginning with accumulating resources in anticipation of adverse life events—in keeping with the old adage "A stitch in time saves nine." The resources can be anything from money to social support to simply being organized and able to plan ahead. Another step in proactive coping is recognizing the signs that a challenge might be on the horizon, such as having to send children to college, or a possible layoff at work. Foreseeing these things leads you to make primary appraisals about the level of threat and the extent of action that might be necessary now to prevent the event from being a major life stressor. At this point, active coping begins; you take concrete steps to protect your interests against the foreseen problem. In this way, you avoid stress proactively rather than reacting to it.

Deliberately choosing proactive coping gives you more control over your reaction to potentially stressful life events. Proactive coping can serve you well in many ways. First, it motivates you to adopt a more active coping style in general. There is abundant evidence that active coping, in response to most stressors, is highly adaptive and helpful in maintaining a good quality of life. Adopting a proactive coping style gives you practice in using active coping techniques, which helps you become more adept at deciding when and where to use each strategy. Being practiced at active coping strategies makes it easier to recognize when *not* to use them—for instance, in the face of an uncontrollable situation.

Another benefit of proactive coping is that it guides you in reframing prior stressful experiences and putting them to good use. Your past mistakes and problems become learning opportunities. We've all heard (or perhaps said), "I'll never do *that* again!" Well, this is a form of proactive coping, or at least an early step. The next steps involve making a logical plan that will prevent you from having to cope with that particular stressor over and over again.

Healthy Coping Strategies

As you'll remember, secondary appraisals—deciding whether you can exert any control to improve a situation and evaluating whether you can cope with it—involve a thinking component and a feeling component. This is also true of coping strategies. Some responses to stressful events are primarily cognitive; others are more emotional. Over and over again, all day, you are using some combination of cognitive and emotional strategies, often without even knowing you're doing it. Imagine how much more effective you can be if you cultivate a variety of coping skills and learn when, where, and how to use them. We'll start by looking at problem-solving techniques, and then we'll look at strategies for managing the emotional consequences of stressful events. Finally, we'll consider a third approach to coping, known as meaning-based coping, that can take the idea of simply reacting to and dealing with stressors into the realm of personal growth and life mastery.

PROBLEM SOLVING

Problem-solving coping skills are most appropriate in situations over which you have at least some control. Problem solving is a logical response when your secondary appraisal tells you yes, there's something you can do about what's happening to make it less of a threat. Some examples of problem solving include goal setting, organization, planning, information seeking, and mental simulation. Each of these strategies is helpful because it involves confronting a problem head-on and exerting some personal control in the situation. Let's consider some problem-solving strategies individually.

"PLANFUL" PROBLEM SOLVING. Making a plan to confront a problem serves several important purposes. First, it helps you define the problem in concrete terms and tends to bring the possible negative outcomes down to earth. Also, it gives you a greater sense of control over the problem, if only over your own emotional responses. This is often helpful when you find yourself mulling something over repeatedly and getting nowhere. Try taking pen to paper and writing down a series of steps you can take to address the problem. Start by brainstorming. Allow yourself to be unrealistic, fanciful, and even playful in the steps you could take. These sessions can uncover ideas you otherwise wouldn't have thought of, leading you to a different approach than you're used to—one that might be more successful. At the very least, you will have an idea of the extent of your control over the situation, which can help you decide if you really should act now or perhaps pursue emotional comfort until the situation changes.

CONFRONTIVE COPING. You can think of this as sticking up for yourself. It's a technique that comes naturally to some, but for many people, it's hard to do. Taken to an extreme, this type of coping can alienate people and pose a risk to your social support network. The key is to direct your confrontational energy where it will be most helpful. If you're upset with your boss, communicate your concerns directly rather than taking your frustration out on your coworkers. Interpersonal confrontation is a delicate art that requires strong emotional regulation. It's at the times when you feel most indignant and victimized that you need to use the most restraint in confronting the person who has harmed you. Used effectively, this technique can go a long way to resolving feelings of helplessness, and it can give you a sense of being in control of what happens to you. In chapter 7, you will learn helpful ways to express strong negative emotions, and in chapter 8, you will learn about using social interaction skillfully to manage challenges.

INFORMATION SEEKING. This is an active coping technique that can alleviate stress by reducing uncertainty. It's generally considered a helpful approach, especially when the stressor is a health problem, but there are some caveats. First, information seeking may work best for challenges that are short-term, and for which information is readily available. For longer-term stressors, an emphasis on information seeking can lead to a type of hypervigilance that can become stressful in itself. If information is elusive or simply not available, like the outcome of an upcoming medical test, it is probably not helpful to spend a lot of time gathering information about all the possible outcomes without knowing the results of the testing. This is an example of an uncontrollable stressor that may call for emotional regulation rather than a more active approach.

MENTAL SIMULATION. This is a form of imagery, which I'll explain in detail in chapter 9. Mental simulation is seeing, feeling, and imagining yourself successfully managing a stressful situation. In a relaxed state, you can take yourself through the event (for example, a major exam or a scary confrontation with someone) and see yourself staying calm, making good choices, and avoiding harm. This is a form of rehearsal, and it can be helpful in a couple of ways. First, it helps you see what aspects of this challenge you can control and change. Second, it helps you accept the possibility of a good outcome. You can strengthen this by using repeated sessions of mental simulation. Also, simulation helps you figure out what resources you'll need to draw upon (your sense of humor, your sense of justice, your ability to concentrate) when the time comes. Imagery techniques are useful in a variety of situations, and they're some of the best ways to manage stress both in the moment and in the anticipation of an event.

SEEKING INSTRUMENTAL SOCIAL SUPPORT. There are many types of social support, and most of them are highly beneficial when you're under stress. *Instrumental social support* is practical help when you need it. Perhaps you need a ride to the hospital, or a short-term loan, or a car for some errands. Having one or more people in your life whom you can count on for these things is a real benefit. Family members can provide social support as a matter of course, but for the most part, it is a resource that you need to look for and cultivate. You can read more about social support in chapter 8, but in short, you can cope better if you have people in your life who will help you.

EMOTION-FOCUSED COPING

It's been said that all stressors require both problem-focused coping and emotion-focused coping. This is probably true, but different types of stressors call for different coping approaches. When a situation is a threat that is mostly, if not completely, out of your control, sometimes your only recourse is to manage your emotional responses and ride it out—until it passes, until the situation changes in a way that allows you to be more active, or, in some cases, for the rest of your life. It's very important to be able to minimize your level of emotional distress in the face of stress without denying or suppressing your thoughts and feelings. This is why it's worthwhile to cultivate and practice emotion-based coping skills.

SEEKING EMOTIONAL SOCIAL SUPPORT. Emotional social support comes in the form of someone in your life whom you trust, whom you can talk to about your problems. This helps in so many ways. First, it gives you a feeling of connectedness that helps avert loneliness. Loneliness is recognized as a risk factor for illness and premature death. Second, emotional social support helps you create a logical story about the problem and make a realistic assessment of the resources available to you for coping.

ACCESSING AND VENTING EMOTIONS. Emotions can take on a life of their own. They certainly can change the state of your body. Anger and frustration can increase blood pressure and heart rate to dangerous levels. Sadness to the point of depression can compromise immune function. Suppressing emotion is a form of avoidant coping that can be harmful to your health. The key to emotional venting is to allow a free flow of what you're feeling but to avoid getting preoccupied with the emotional consequences of the problem at the expense of working on solving the problem. A healthy balance of emotional discharge with rational problem solving is a highly effective way to deal with stress.

Physical exercise is an extremely good method of discharging emotional energy. Sadly, many people who normally engage in regular physical exercise often stop working out when they're in a stressful period. This robs them of a resource that's helpful in regulating emotion, maintaining cardiovascular and immune health, and maintaining self-esteem just when they really need it. So, if you exercise regularly, don't let your routine fall by the wayside when you're under stress. That's the time you need it the most. In chapter 6, we'll explore the benefits of body awareness and movement. This may be especially helpful to you if exercise is not a part of your life now.

MEANING-BASED COPING

Meaning-based coping is a set of skills more recently recognized as effective coping tools. It's a way to seek personal growth and wisdom through life's difficult times. Getting through a struggle can give you a stronger sense of your own strength and more appreciation for your inner resources.

POSITIVE REINTERPRETATION AND GROWTH. Finding the silver lining in a dark cloud can be a blessing. It's possible to look at stress and problems as learning experiences, even when you endure a great loss. This becomes easier when you cultivate an attitude of acceptance of things you can't control. Giving up your inbred sense of omnipotence frees you from feeling you have to control everything. From this perspective, loss and hardship are things to be accepted and endured; the choice is yours to grow from it or feel a sense of defeat. Many of life's struggles can be reinterpreted as opportunities to see life from a different perspective, to learn to accept change and be more flexible, and to think of yourself as a survivor rather than a victim. Finding meaning in your life has been shown to be protective against depression (Mascaro and Rosen 2006). Women who use this strategy tend to have less cardiovascular reactivity in stress-provoking situations (Fontana and Badawy 1997).

TURNING TO RELIGION OR SPIRITUALITY. The physical and mental health benefits of religiousness and spirituality have been documented extensively in the recent medical literature. Part of these benefits seems to come from the way a transcendent perspective on life helps people cope with problems. Putting everyday issues into a larger perspective helps them seem smaller and more manageable. Allowing for the possibility that your life is part of something bigger can give your successes and good deeds more importance and enhance your feelings of self-worth. In addition, religion is often practiced within a community, such as a church, and these communities provide a great deal of social support to their members. Chapter 10 addresses a variety of ways that you can use meaning and spirituality to empower yourself to manage stress better, whether you're religious or not.

MAKING COMPARISONS. No matter how bad things get, it's always possible to imagine that someone else is worse off than you are, or that things could get worse. This may seem like morbid thinking, but it can actually be beneficial to a certain degree (Thompson 1985). It lends a tone of hope to what you're dealing with, and it can even spark a feeling of good fortune. If your house burns down, at least nobody was hurt. If you lose a breast to cancer, at least you're still alive. If you lose your job, at least you have your health. If you don't make enough money to take a great vacation, at least you earn enough to keep your home. Thoughts like these can help you stay engaged in active coping because you're thinking about the problem without being defeated by it. If you find a kernel of good fortune in the fact that things aren't worse, you're allowing room for emotional soothing and proactive coping as well as direct problem solving.

FINDING SIDE BENEFITS. In her book *Shattered Assumptions* (1992), Ronnie Janoff-Bulman explores the ways major stressors can change a person's worldview. She describes several processes of adaptation to and integration of traumatic events. One thing many people do is find side benefits to the disaster, like the way that adversity can deepen and strengthen relationships. You can learn from the bad things that happen to you. You can become more appreciative of the good things in your life. You can learn to embrace every day that you're given. All of these side benefits and more are the hidden gifts of stress and trauma, and it's up to you to find and appreciate them.

Conclusion

The major take-home lesson from the research on stress and coping is that you can best take care of yourself by paying attention to your individual coping style and the appraisals you make about the events in your life. This gives you the power to choose how you think about your life, to control your reactions to events, and even to avoid stress before it happens using proactive coping. All of these add up to more happiness, personal growth, and peace in every day.

Use Your Strengths to Your Advantage

In January 2000, an entire issue of *American Psychologist*, the peer-reviewed journal of the American Psychological Association, was devoted to the new and blossoming field of *positive psychology*, the study of the strengths and virtues of the human being. This field is generating important research and becoming widely accepted as an alternate view of psychology. It shifts the focus away from distress and pathology and toward what makes a healthy, productive, happy human being and how these things can be instilled and nurtured in all of us. Positive psychology has catalogued and developed assessments for many human strengths, but we're going to focus on a few: optimism, self-efficacy, and choosing to be happy. Before we look at each of these strengths, let's take a closer look at the tenets of positive psychology.

Understanding Positive Psychology

David Buss (2000) wrote about an evolutionary perspective on human development that sheds interesting light on the sources of stress and unhappiness in modern life. Buss pointed out that human beings have lived in industrialized environments for only a couple of centuries. For millennia before this, we lived entirely different lives, to which we were very well adapted. This preindustrial life included the need to do physical work to acquire food; living in small groups with extended family; simpler, less alluring demands on attention from day to day; an absence of mass media and engineered imagery pulling us out of our immediate experience; and less of the social alienation that comes from mobility and large communities.

If Buss is correct, and the human psyche developed for thousands of years to cope with simpler, more socially connected lives committed to caring for the home and getting food to eat, then the complexity and speed of life today is something we're not optimally suited for.

Cultivating Strengths and Virtues to Cope with Stress

Recently, Chris Peterson and Martin Seligman (2004) published a book that sums up the research in positive psychology so far, in the form of a handbook and classification of human strengths and virtues. This book represents an extremely systematic and scholarly approach to understanding and encouraging the basic strengths and gifts that each of us is born with and can, to some extent, develop more fully. The focus is not on depression, anxiety, and other things that go wrong; there are plenty of manuals about that. This area of psychology is dedicated to figuring out what people do well and how to build on that to help individuals and societies become happier and more constructive.

What does this have to do with stress management? Being happy and being debilitated by stress are incompatible states of being. There is no way to avoid stress and challenge in life, but it is entirely possible to maintain a sense of happiness and well-being even in the most difficult circumstances.

Enduring and meeting challenges can give you a sense of deep satisfaction and trust in yourself. This can sustain you through the next challenge and the next, so that as you age and life continues to change, you gain in resiliency and wisdom, and you find hidden gifts in many if not most of life's challenges and losses.

What are the basic human strengths Peterson and Seligman catalogued in their manual? They fall into six major categories:

- wisdom and knowledge

- courage

- humanity

- justice

- temperance

- transcendence

Each of these categories has several components. For example, under courage, you find bravery, persistence, integrity, and vitality. These are lofty ideas about human character that hearken back to a less cynical age. Yet they are more relevant than ever, as the world becomes more complicated and more interconnected. It's vital that you let go of a bit of your cynicism and consider what it is within you that creates a world of fairness, kindness, and happiness. After all, what else is there to strive for?

Let's focus on the virtues and strengths that are most useful in coping with stress.

OPTIMISM

Optimism is a stance toward life that continually allows for good outcomes. In recent years, it has been linked to better health, better performance at work and school, longer life, and more happiness. But what is optimism, how does it help you, and how can you become more optimistic and reap the benefits?

Defining Optimism

Chris Peterson (2000) from the University of Michigan describes optimism as a combination of thought and emotion with a component of motivation. One consistent notion of optimism is the tendency to have positive expectations for the future, to expect good outcomes. Peterson suggests that defined this way, optimism is a good predictor of a person's use of active coping, which tends to be particularly effective and less conducive to emotional distress.

The Benefits of Optimism

Optimism seems to exert its benefits in several ways. One is through its effects on mood. People who can endure stress and still maintain a positive emotional tone reap many rewards. Good mood seems to go along with better flexibility in thinking about your options, and it promotes generosity and social responsibility, thus enhancing social connections (Isen 2003). In general, optimists have fewer episodes of bad moods in the face of stress when compared to pessimists (Carver and Scheier 2002).

Another benefit of optimism appears to be a reduction in the bad effects of stress on the immune system. This was borne out in the results of a study of students coping with their first year of law school (Segerstrom et al. 1998). The law students who were optimistic tended to have better moods and better immune functioning as the year progressed, especially the students who demonstrated *situational optimism*, that is, an optimistic attitude toward doing well in law school. The link between optimism and immune function was also observed in a study of men with human immunodeficiency virus (HIV). Men in the study who were optimistic—even to the extent that they had unrealistically positive expectations about the outcome of their disease—had slower progression of their disease than men with pessimistic outlooks (Taylor et al. 2000). The progression of disease with HIV is strongly affected by changes in immune function.

The bad effects of pessimism on health may be greater than the positive effects of optimism. According to research by Jagdish Dua (1994) of the University of New England in Australia, the best predictor of psychological and physical problems is negative moods resulting from pessimistic thinking. Dua also observed that how people explain the bad events in their lives is a more important predictor of health than how they explain the good events. So it makes sense to take a look at how you explain the bad things that happen to you, and to see if you can adopt a more optimistic way of thinking about them.

Another way that optimism is helpful is by inspiring people to engage in more self-care. This effect was observed by Taylor and colleagues (2000) in a study of men with HIV. The optimistic men tended to take better care of themselves. Optimism may also help by enhancing social relationships. There are many health benefits to social support, and optimism, with its attendant positive mood states, may encourage people to create and sustain more supportive relationships with others.

Optimism and Explanatory Style

Optimists can be defined by the way they explain the things that happen to them. *Explanatory style* has been studied extensively as a way to predict a person's health and happiness in the present and in the future. Explanatory style includes three dimensions. The first, *internality*, concerns whether events have happened or will happen as a result of you and your actions, or whether they're determined by the will or actions of others (or fate). The second dimension, *stability*, considers whether the current situation is caused by factors that are stable and long lasting or temporary and transient. The third aspect of explanatory style is *globality*; this refers to whether the cause of a good or bad event is case specific or applies to all aspects of your life.

When something bad happens, an optimist tends to explain it in terms of causes that are external to the self (not internal), transient (not stable), and specific to the situation (not global). A pessimistic person would make the opposite attributions. In their study of university students in their freshman year, Chris Peterson and Lisa Barrett (1987) found that those students who had a more pessimistic explanatory style tended to get lower grades at school when compared to the students with more optimistic explanatory styles. Research has also shown that pessimistic explanatory style is present in people who have higher rates of depression (Peterson and Seligman 1984).

Here's an example of optimism at work: I'm driving to work on a rainy day. I'm running a little late, so I'm hurrying but not speeding. On a bend in the road, I skid out and end up with my car in the ditch. As an optimist, I explain the situation this way: *The road is slippery* (low internality) *because it's raining today* (low stability). *This bend in the road is particularly sharp and hard to navigate when the road is slippery* (low globality). Now let's look at how a pessimist would explain the same situation: *I was driving too fast because I didn't manage my time well today* (high internality). *I am always running late* (high stability), *and this is only one of the stupid things that have happened because I'm so bad at managing my time* (high globality).

Can you learn to be more optimistic? Research suggests that you can. To cultivate an attitude of optimism, take a critical look at your own explanatory style. When something bad happens, pay attention to your thoughts. Do you assume that the situation happened because of something about you or something you did? Is it something that "always" happens to you? Is it just one example of the kind of thing that happens to you? Ask yourself if there's another possible explanation that's external, transient, and specific to the situation.

SELF-EFFICACY: THE CONFIDENCE TO THRIVE

Self-efficacy is the belief that even in the most difficult circumstances, you can take care of yourself. It's the conviction that you have some control over the events of your life. This quality goes hand in hand with optimism. Where optimism helps you develop your expectations for the future, building self-efficacy can improve your confidence that you are capable of meeting those expectations, even when things are hard to handle. Self-efficacy is situation specific; that is, you can have high self-efficacy about your capabilities as a student but low self-efficacy in the area of romantic relationships.

The effect of self-efficacy on health and stress has been studied extensively. In their study of emotional self-efficacy and quality of life, Gian Caprara and Patizia Steca (2005) found that people who feel confident about their ability to express positive emotion and manage negative emotion tended to engage in more positive thinking and to have higher levels of life satisfaction and optimism. High levels of self-efficacy can help you have a good quality of life, even in the face of a disease, as Connie Kohler and Larry Fish (2002) found in their study of people with emphysema. In these patients, having high self-efficacy for taking care of themselves went along with actually doing better clinically and having a better quality of life.

Having high self-efficacy motivates you to work harder and be more persistent in reaching your goals. The good news is that you can learn to have more self-efficacy in any area of your life. How do you do this? There are several well-documented ways. The first step is to be very specific about what you want to feel more confident about. This is often easiest if you think of it in terms of a goal. Let's say you want to start exercising regularly. Begin by setting a goal that is realistic given your current fitness level and your schedule. Suppose you want to take a thirty-minute walk three times a week. How can you build your self-efficacy with respect to that goal, and thereby increase your chances of accomplishing it? Here's how:

PROVIDE YOURSELF WITH THE EXPERIENCE OF SUCCESS. Set small goals that gradually build to your ultimate desired outcome. Only when you accomplish the smaller goals should you progress to bigger ones. So, it would be helpful to start by walking five minutes once a week, or whatever increment you know for sure you can do. Once you've mastered that, you have added to your sense of confidence, and you can take on a bigger challenge.

LIVE VICARIOUSLY. Find examples of people like you who have accomplished similar goals. You can do this by reading personal stories in fitness magazines, doing some social networking, or simply going to exercise classes or the track and looking for people you identify with. You want to trigger the *If he can do it, so can I* feeling. You can seek out vicarious experience by simply asking people how they do it. It's a great way to meet people, and in the process, you're actually helping the person you're asking, because you're reinforcing their success for them.

LET YOURSELF BE PERSUADED. You think you need to get more exercise to be healthier? Why not ask your doctor what she thinks? I can almost guarantee you that she will help you by telling you it's a great idea. Getting input and encouragement from people you trust and admire for their expertise or experience is a well-documented promoter of self-efficacy.

PAY ATTENTION TO HOW YOU FEEL. Something inside you is motivating you to take up walking. What is it? Do you feel anxious about your health and the possible consequences of being out of shape? Pay attention to that anxiety and see how much better you feel after you take that walk. You have taken care of your anxiety about the activity by simply doing it. It's another benefit of taking action to make yourself happier and manage your stress. Over time, many people find that it's easier to just get out there and take the walk or go to the gym than it is to manage the discomfort that comes from knowing you've let yourself down. The key is to pay attention to these feelings as they come up, allow them to be, and choose the course of least stress.

CHOOSING TO BE HAPPY

Happiness can be seen as a choice you make in life. For many people, it's the only thing really worth striving for. There's a difference between a life of pleasure and short-term gratification and a life of long-term gratification, satisfaction, and well-being. Focusing on your strengths is one way to cultivate true happiness. Looking at the research on happiness, Jason Satterfield (2001) from the University of California, San Francisco made the following observations:

- Happiness seems to occur most often in people who have good social support, are married, have religion or spirituality in their lives, and tend to be more extroverted than introverted.

- Unhappiness seems to occur more often in people who value money, status, prestige, and occupational success than in people who value relationships above all other things.

- Things that seem to have little or no effect on a person's happiness include age, gender, income (above the level at which the most basic needs are met), and physical attractiveness.

Here's an interesting exercise to try. First, make a list of the things you think are most important in life, in your heart and mind and ideals. Number these priorities and arrange them in a list with the most important at the top. Next, think about your average week. Make a list of broad categories of what you do during the week: working, watching television, being with your family, going to church, and so on. Now, arrange this list with the activity that takes the most time at the top and the one that takes the least time at the bottom. Compare your two lists. Are you spending enough time on the things you value most? Of course, you probably have to work, and so your job likely scores high in terms of time spent. Embedded in your work is probably your desire to provide for your family, maintain social ties, and give yourself intellectual stimulation, along with other goals that serve your higher purposes. It's especially valuable to consider how you use your time outside of work. Think about whether what you do in your free time aligns with what you truly care about. A mismatch here can be a source of stress that you might not have recognized because so many behaviors are simply habits, not conscious acts flowing from higher goals.

In 2005, Martin Seligman and his colleagues published data from a study in which they developed an Internet-based intervention to improve happiness and reduce depressive symptoms in a group of people. They recommended one of several happiness-inducing exercises to participants, and compared the results of those exercises to a more neutral exercise. Over time, the people who tried the happiness-promoting exercises had an improvement in mood and feelings of well-being. Try some of these exercises for yourself, and see if you reap the same benefits.

Exercise: Building Happiness

First, write a page in your notebook about how you've been feeling for the last couple of weeks. After you've written for a few minutes, stop and answer these questions in your notebook. Use a scale of 1 to 10, with 1 being rotten and 10 being fantastic.

1. Overall, how happy have you been?

2. Overall, how well have you been getting along with the people close to you?

3. How have you been sleeping?

4. How well have you been taking care of your health needs?

5. What are your expectations for your life in the next month or so?

6. What are your expectations for your life in the next year or two?

7. How would you rate your overall quality of life?

Now, put these responses aside. During the next week, do one of the following activities:

GRATITUDE VISIT. Write a letter of gratitude to a person who has been especially kind to you and whom you feel you haven't properly thanked. After you've written the letter, deliver it in person.

THREE GOOD THINGS IN LIFE. Every night, sit down with your journal and write down three things that went well that day. In addition, write down the causes of each of these good things. Then write a brief explanation of the cause of each good thing. For example, *Today I gave a good lecture to my class. It was good because I was well prepared. I was well prepared because I managed my time efficiently enough to make it possible to put extra effort into the presentation.*

YOU AT YOUR BEST. In your notebook, write a story about a time in your life when you were at your absolute best. Make it about a page long, and go into detail about why you were at your best. You might mention things like work, relationships, and health. Then, every day for a week, reread the story and reflect on the strengths inherent in your story.

USE YOUR STRENGTHS. Go to www.authentic happiness.org and take the inventory of character strengths. When you get the results, make a list of your top five strengths in your notebook. Over the next week, see if you can consciously use these strengths as often as possible in your daily life.

At the end of the week, repeat the seven questions you answered before trying the exercise. If you noticed a difference, you're like many of the people in the study. People got the most benefit from the three good things exercise and the gratitude visit, but all of the exercises provided at least some benefit. If you like, you can spend another week on another exercise or try a couple at once.

Conclusion

This chapter has offered you a way to cope with stress by focusing more on your strengths and abilities and less on your shortcomings and insecurities. What you focus on tends to become more active in your life, so it makes sense to recognize, embrace, and nurture your own innate gifts. You can further explore the idea of virtues and strengths by visiting the positive psychology Web site www.viastrengths.org.

Get Into the Flow of Life

Sometimes it seems that life comes at you in a rush. One day follows the next, and before you realize it, another week has gone by, then a month, and then a year. The older you get, the more pronounced this sense of life flashing by becomes. In itself, this change in your sense of time can become stressful in practical ways, but it's also stressful in the existential sense. It can create a kind of despair to feel your life slipping away without your being able to enjoy, savor, and deeply experience it. Children grow from babies to adolescents to young adults, and you ask yourself where the time goes. Surely there must be a way, in the midst of all you have to do, to slow down and be in the flow of life as it's happening, without waiting until one of your two weeks of vacation every year. The good news is that, yes, there are ways you can rein in the rush of time and be fully present in every day. The two most powerful ways I know of to do that are seeking flow and cultivating mindfulness.

Flow

Let's begin by exploring the idea of flow.

WHAT IS FLOW?

Flow is the state of being in which creativity occurs. In his book *Finding Flow* (1997), Mihaly Csikszentmihalyi expands on his several years of research on highly creative people from many different spheres of life to explain how every person can bring more experiences of peak creativity into everyday life. Csikszentmihalyi describes flow as a state of optimal experience, when "what we feel, what we wish, and what we think are in harmony" (29).

Flow can happen during many different activities. Have you ever been so involved in doing something that you lost track of time? One moment flows into the next, and you're thinking, but only about what you're doing. You're not distracted by worries about the future or regrets from the past. This is truly blissful, being in the here and now, fully focused. In my life, I have experienced flow while nursing my babies, skiing down big mountains, rock climbing, and playing the piano. Dancing is another way that I access flow.

Take a moment and ask yourself what things you have done that engaged your full attention in a pleasurable, rhythmic way, without being stressful. In your journal, write down a few of the best moments of your life. Pick the top three, and see if you can describe what made them so good, besides the objective circumstances. How did you experience your body during those times? What was your perception of time? Did it seem to slow down or speed up? What was your emotional state? How did things register to your senses—visually, auditorily, by touch, taste, and smell? In a moment, we'll look at Csikszentmihalyi's explanation of the flow state, and you can check back and see what aspects of your personal peak experiences correspond to his thinking about flow.

Flow state has several characteristic qualities. They refer to the task that a person is engaged in and to the state the person enters while performing the task. Let's consider each of these characteristics.

Clear Goals

In flow, you always know what needs to be done; for example, the musician knows what notes to play next. There is a great deal of evidence in the social and health psychology literature that having goals promotes health. This is, in part, because long- and short-term goals lead to immediate intentions, and, according to some theorists, intention is the most important determinant of behavior. From a more philosophic perspective, goals are beneficial because they give form to your experiences. As a rock climber, I always have as my goal reaching the top of the route I'm climbing. I have that goal because it's what motivates me to stretch myself and apply my skills to ascending the rock. Without that goal, I would still climb, but I wouldn't have the experience of pushing myself beyond my prior limitations to a new level of experience.

Goals in flow psychology do not operate as reasons for self-flagellation in the face of failure. Goals create structure for your experiences, but actually accomplishing them is not the reason for engaging in the activity. This idea will be more clear when we look at the idea of *autotelic*, or inherently valuable, experiences—things done for their own sake, not for a predetermined outcome. It's a lovely paradox, really, balancing the act of setting goals for structure without being strongly attached to the outcome of flow activities. This is what happens when the reason for doing something is the doing, not the end result.

Immediate Feedback

In order to stay engaged in a process, whether it's at work or at play, you need to know how you're doing. In some arenas, like academia, this information is easy to come by—for example, in the form of grades. In other endeavors, the feedback has to come from within. Setting goals creates an opportunity to give yourself feedback. Put simply, you shoot for running two miles today, and if you accomplish that, you're in for some positive mental feedback. But this idea goes deeper than that. You can gain feedback constantly if you maintain a posture of mindfulness in the things you do.

Balance Between Challenge and Skills

In order for an activity to trigger the flow state, it has to offer an optimal balance between the level of challenge and your skills. When you're in flow, you're neither frustrated nor bored. We've all experienced being bored while doing something; time drags on and resentment grows. We've all also been frustrated by tasks that just seemed too complicated or required skills we don't have. Plumbing, for instance, is my downfall. I love to do home improvement projects, but ask me to replace a faucet and my hair stands up.

This is not to say that you should only attempt things you're good at. This leads to stagnation, which runs counter to flow, creativity, and personal growth. What's ideal is to be riding the edge of your abilities as often as possible—at work, home, and play. Goal setting and feedback are part of this as well. Something as simple as emptying the dishwasher can be flow-enhancing if you set the goal to get it done as smoothly and efficiently as possible, paying close attention to the sounds, sights, smells, and sensations of the experience. No, your skill level probably won't advance if you use this approach for tedious chores, but the mental state you achieve while you're doing what you have to do anyway will be higher and more pleasant, and you will feel less stressed about your chores.

Merging of Action and Awareness

In flow, action and awareness are merged. You are in the moment, fully mindful of what you are doing. We're going to focus on mindfulness later in this chapter, but for now, consider the possibility that you can pay attention to what's happening to your body, mind, and spirit all day long, as you go about all the things you do, and by doing so, you'll find more pleasure and meaning in these activities—even loading the dishwasher. Mindfulness serves flow because the feedback loop is tighter and more self-integrated. You start to run; you notice how you're breathing, how your legs feel, and how the trees are swaying slightly in the breeze. You modify your gait, mindfully, based on how you're feeling. No assessment, criticism, or self-bashing is involved. It's a matter of simple awareness combined with small accommodations in what you're doing. This interplay of awareness and action is fundamental to getting into flow.

No Distraction

In the flow state, distractions are excluded from consciousness, because a person in flow is engaged in intense concentration on the present. When you embrace the present moment this way, you are relieved of nagging fears, performance anxiety, and worries about the past or future. This is the true essence of peace of mind, wherein the only thing that matters is what's right in front of you, right now, and you can deal with it, no matter how tedious or scary it might be.

No Self-Consciousness

What a wonderful idea, to be so involved in what you're doing that you stop worrying about how your hair looks or whether you sound stupid or whether you look fat. In flow, this debilitating self-consciousness disappears. The constant self-criticism, which can be very stressful, stops. Paradoxically, we become more competent, more relaxed, and therefore more attractive and easy to be with. There's an epidemic of self-focus in our society that often verges on narcissism. Many people walk around with the basic feeling *It's all about me*. This attitude can grow to a form of self-obsession that creates a lot of stress. Studies of happiness have shown that an outward, non-self-directed attitude is healthier than habitual focus on the self (Compton 2001; Mor and Winquist 2002).

Distorted Sense of Time

During flow, your sense of time becomes distorted. You can be lost in a moment that seems to last forever, or you can look up from a project and realize that hours have passed. This is not the same thing as zoning out in front of the television. In his book *Authentic Happiness* (2002), Martin Seligman differentiates between pleasure and gratification. *Gratification*, Seligman explains, is the sense of well-being that comes from activities done in the state of flow. Gratification, in contrast to pleasure, induces growth and personal development beyond the simple experience of positive feelings. Unfortunately, many people feel too overwhelmed or tired to seek experiences that bring gratification, and settle for pleasure instead. In the long run, if you focus your efforts on pleasure (sitting in front of the television) instead of gratification (throwing a softball around with the kids), you deprive yourself of innumerable opportunities for flow and happiness.

Autotelic Experience

Living life in flow means transforming more and more of your daily tasks from things you have to do to things you want to do. The doing—not the result—becomes the thing. That is autotelic experience. This word, which comes from the Greek, means that something is an end in itself. Some activities—such as art, music, and sports—are usually autotelic; there is no reason for doing them except to feel the experience they provide. Most tasks in life are, on the surface, *exotelic*; you do them not because you enjoy them but in order to get at some later goal. And some activities—such as performing surgery or being a concert violinist—are both.

In many ways, the secret to a happy life is to learn to get flow from as many mundane or obligatory things as possible. If work and family life become autotelic, then there is nothing wasted in life, and everything you do is worth doing for its own sake. You still have to do it, but finding flow in the process allows you to avoid feeling that you're wasting your precious time and that your life would have so much more meaning if only you were painting or traveling instead of sitting in this car, driving your children to school.

It's easy to think that autotelic activity is simply a matter of making the best of a bad situation. But what you're doing is not only adjusting to less-than-perfect circumstances. You're reframing your assessment of the situation to allow it to be as it is without giving it a grade. This is a basic principle of mindfulness. Autotelic living doesn't grant constant happiness, but people who live this way tend to report higher levels of purpose, meaning, and positivity in their lives overall (Csikszentmihalyi 1997). As Csikszentmihalyi writes, "People are happy not because of what they do, but because of how they do it" (826). You can start managing stress and finding more peace of mind right now, simply by making changes in how you do the things you do each and every day.

FINDING FLOW IN EVERY DAY

Flow isn't something you are taught; it's a state that your body and mind want to be in. Daily routines, stress, urban lifestyles, passive entertainment, and a host of other factors have severely depleted the amount of time that people spend in flow, but, as you've seen, you have some control over whether you're in flow. You can start slowly, gradually shifting your way of doing things out of automatic habits, drudgery, and anxious business and into flow.

Begin with one task you do each day. To make it easy, choose something you do in your free time, for fun. Chances are, you already experience some degree of flow while doing that. Next time you go for a walk or play a musical instrument or work on your hobby, pay attention to each of the dimensions of flow: goals, feedback, and absorption. Notice what it is about the activity that pleases you. Seek flow by allowing yourself to become immersed in the activity with no distractions. Next, try doing this with another task, one that doesn't usually bring you a lot of joy, like paying your bills or washing the kitchen floor. Again, see if you can apply some of the principles of flow to this activity. Keep at it, and it will begin to come naturally, because you are hardwired for flow. It's simply a matter of getting your busy mind out of the way so you can experience life directly.

Mindfulness

Mindfulness is an aspect of flow, but it stands on its own as a way of experiencing life in the present moment.

WHAT IS MINDFULNESS?

In simplest terms, *mindfulness* is the act of paying attention to your life as it unfolds, without placing value judgments on anything that happens. Birds flying in the air, children playing outside, the taste of macaroni and cheese—these are all things to be allowed, to be noted and attended to, but not to be assessed for their essential goodness or badness. It's a natural human tendency to judge and evaluate everything around us. It's a basic survival instinct that often serves us well. It's good to know when to trust someone, when to avoid a certain street or to avoid drinking too much. There are things in the world that can harm us, and we do ourselves a service by recognizing them and avoiding them. Being mindful is not walking around in a perpetual state of bliss, examining each flower as if the secrets of the universe lay within it.

Mindfulness is a here-and-now, hands-on approach to living that makes daily life richer and more instructive. If you approach life as a learning experience, an opportunity to grow and move toward wisdom and grace, you will almost certainly become a more mindful person. Mindfulness comes from Eastern philosophy and practice, and it is frequently associated with Buddhist meditation. Some of the most prominent teachers and writers on mindfulness come from the Buddhist tradition, but as you'll see, it's a quality of life that belongs to everyone, a natural part of human existence. There is nothing inherent in mindfulness that is anti-Christian, anti-Jewish, or sectarian. Most religious traditions have a type of contemplation or meditation as part of their legacy, but practicing mindfulness can be a strictly secular pursuit as well.

Philosophy aside, there has been a tremendous amount of research into the effects of mindfulness and mindfulness-based stress reduction on overall health and well-being. The data are fascinating and offer guidance in how to live each day, regardless of religious or spiritual orientation. Mindfulness is a skill that can help you slow down, cue in, and be an active participant in every moment of your life.

In his landmark book *Full Catastrophe Living* (1990), Jon Kabat-Zinn applied the concept of mindfulness to stress management. He started leading mindfulness-based stress reduction groups at the University of Massachusetts in the late 1970s and is an authority in the field, training patients and medical professionals all over the world in the use of mindfulness meditation as a way to reduce stress and live a healthier life. In *Full Catastrophe Living*, Kabat-Zinn sums up the potential benefits of mindfulness: shifting from doing to being, making time for yourself, nurturing calmness and self-acceptance, observing your mind from moment to moment, letting thoughts go without getting caught up in their content, making room for new insights and approaches to problems, and seeing how everything is connected to everything else.

Herbert Benson at Harvard Medical School has developed, researched, and written about meditation for stress management. In *The Relaxation Response* (1975), Benson teaches a state of calm, detached awareness associated with positive changes in the nervous, cardiovascular, and other systems of the body. The basic event in the relaxation response is deactivation of the fight-or-flight mechanism, allowing the body and mind to be relaxed, giving the entire system a break from the continual barrage of stress physiology that so many of us experience.

The purpose of this chapter is not to train you in mindfulness meditation, but to orient you to a mindful way of being in everything you do. However, if you're so inclined, you can find meditation workshops and classes in many communities in the United States, and it can become a valuable part of your stress management program.

THE BENEFITS OF MINDFULNESS MEDITATION

There is a growing body of evidence that mindfulness-based stress reduction, which includes daily meditation practice, can benefit health. Many studies have shown mindfulness meditation to be useful for people with chronic pain (Kaplan, Goldenberg, and Galvin-Nadeau 1993; Kabat-Zinn et al. 1987). Kabat-Zinn and his colleagues (1998) successfully treated patients with psoriasis using mindfulness meditation in conjunction with light therapy; the combination yielded better results than light therapy alone. Psoriasis is strongly linked to stress, and mindfulness meditation reduces the physiology of stress. In the area of mental health, mindfulness meditation has been helpful in reducing the symptoms of emotional distress in chronic pain patients (Astin 1997) and has proved to be effective in managing anxiety disorders (Kabat-Zinn et al. 1992). Mindfulness-based stress reduction also seems to help people manage medical problems long-term with fewer visits to their doctors (Roth and Stanley 2002).

Detachment from Thought Content

In their review of the research on the effects of meditation on the brain, Rael Cahn and John Polich (2006) speculate that one of the reasons meditation helps reduce the symptoms of depression and stress is that it encourages the practitioner to see negative thoughts as something separate from the self. In their article published in 1985, Ilan Kutz, Joan Borysenko, and Herbert Benson describe the ways that detached awareness and emotional regulation, mainstays of mindfulness meditation, parallel the goals of many types of psychotherapy. It seems that these skills—if they're incorporated into daily life— underlie the benefits of talk therapy. If you can observe stressful thinking without making it part of your identity, you can avoid a lot of emotional distress. Simply saying to yourself, *This is only a thought I'm having right now, and it will pass* acknowledges the temporary nature of all thoughts.

Decreasing Emotional Reactivity

Emotional stability goes hand in hand with detaching from the content of your thoughts. Simply giving yourself time between observing a thought and reacting to it can prevent many emotional dips in the course of a single day. The first step is to realize that thoughts are simply content, words, little stories. You can pay attention to them, perhaps even heed them and act on them, but you need not allow them to determine your emotional state. That is something you can practice and get very good at.

Here's an example. I walk into a party and see an old friend I haven't seen for a while. I smile at her, and she gives me a brief wave and goes back to her conversation. A cascade of thoughts goes through my mind, quicker than I can process them, and a moment later I'm feeling sad and rejected. I go on with the evening with that emotion nagging at me. The alternative is to take a second after my friend turns away to tune in to the words I'm saying to myself, without judging or reacting to them. As far as my friend is concerned, what's done is done. It's my job now to examine my thoughts and manage my feelings about what I'm thinking. In fact, I'm not having feelings about what she did or didn't do—I'm having feelings about what I'm *thinking* about what she did, and most of those thoughts flash by so quickly and automatically that I'm not really sure why I feel hurt. So, let's slow down and look at thoughts I might be having: *She doesn't like me any more. We haven't spoken for a while, and it's because she has other friends she likes better. She thinks I'm boring. That other person is more interesting than I am.*

Whether or not any of those things is true doesn't really matter. What matters is that now I'm aware of my thoughts, and I have choices about what I'm going to do with my feelings. I could decide that the thoughts are all true and my feelings are hurt, and go on being sad. I could decide to check these things out with her directly and see if they're true for her. I could decide that it doesn't matter, because the fact is I haven't called her either, and I have other friends I enjoy more. Or maybe she's just being polite to the person she's conversing with, and we'll connect later. All of these things are possible, and by taking a moment to simply observe what has happened and what I'm thinking in response to it, I'm allowing myself to react in a way that's better for me, my friend, and the other people at the party. I'm also taking an important step to protect my own physiology from the whimsies of social slights and embarrassments. By being mindful of my thought content and not judging it (*Oh, that's ridiculous, I'm just being stupid* isn't very helpful either), I am creating breathing room between perception, thinking, and feeling, which gives me control and protection in a wide variety of situations.

HOW TO QUIET YOUR MIND

A quiet mind is a blessing you can grant yourself with practice. Can you remember a time when all you were doing was sitting, and maybe looking? Hearing sounds, sensing your body, feeling your breath, but not creating a narrative about what was happening? Can you remember times when you were simply being, not doing anything—not even meditating or "relaxing"? When you are still but highly observant, not bothered by assessments (good or bad, okay or not okay) but simply allowing everything around you to be what it is, you are in a meditative state. I have found, in my years of leading mind-body groups, that this is a good place for beginners to start exploring the mindful state. I've had wonderful experiences of this in airports, riding in cars (not while I was driving!), while lying in the snow after falling down skiing, and at family gatherings, among other places. Time seems to stand still. I'm quiet on the inside, but acutely observant in a curious, gentle way of everything within and around me. Moments like those convinced me that I could use meditation to calm my sometimes manic mind.

Here is a good way to begin practicing mindfulness. Find a time when you can take ten minutes to yourself. You do not have to be in a darkened room with candles and incense in order to do this. You can be outside, in the lobby of a large office building or a hotel, on your front porch—even in your car, if it's not moving. All you need is to sit and be fairly confident that you won't be interrupted for a few minutes. Now, get comfortable in your seat. Adjust your clothing or glasses so you aren't distracted by anything tugging or compressing parts of your body. Uncross your legs, if you're comfortable with that. With both feet on the ground and your hands in your lap, check your whole body once more to make sure you can relax.

Now, start thinking about the fact that you're breathing. Don't make a big deal out of it. Just notice that *Hey, guess what, there's air flowing in and out of me every few seconds. And the air is a bit cool as it flows into my nose and into my throat. I can feel my chest expanding as the air fills it. As I become more relaxed, I'll feel my belly expanding too. And just at the moment my lungs are full, everything stops for a second, and then I'm exhaling. The air, now warm, is flowing out of me, and my chest is falling.* Just notice this for a minute or so. If your mind wanders away from the miracle that is your breath, just let go of whatever your mind has got its teeth into, and return your attention to the air flowing in and out, in and out. This is a good thing, this breath. It brings life in, and it carries used-up old stuff out. It keeps you fresh from moment to moment. Just keep going back to it, and your mind will gradually stop jumping around.

Now, start to pay attention to what is going on around you. This is a shift you need to make carefully, because you might find your mind flooded with words about what things look like and whether things are okay and what's she wearing? And who did her hair? If this happens, gently return your narrative mind to your breath. Say to yourself, "air in, air out" with the movement of your breath until you can be curiously attentive to the world around you without the running commentary. The goal is to appreciate, perceive, and allow all you see, hear, feel, smell, and sense with a quiet, nonjudgmental mind.

Simple awareness is something humans are born with— babies and toddlers use it all the time. They're just observing. As you practice this, you'll slowly develop the ability to shift into simple awareness a few times each day. It's a very different way of being in the world, one that short-circuits stress because there's no need for self-consciousness, for comparing yourself to other people, for complaining or ruminating over past or future problems.

Eventually, you'll want to make the connection between occasionally practicing simple awareness in the world and practicing it continually with respect to your own thoughts and perceptions. Think about this: You can observe your thoughts and actions the way you observe the world, without constant judgment, and simply allow yourself to be as you are. If you notice things you'd like to change, that's fine, but begin by simply allowing yourself to be, and by cultivating an attitude of friendly curiosity about what's going on in your mind and spirit. This type of self-acceptance is something you have to relearn, because it gets drummed out of you by the culture of materialism and competitiveness, but you can do it.

If you want to deepen your practice and take this farther, perhaps to a sitting meditation, I recommend that you find a meditation teacher. Short of that, the best resource is Thich Nhất Hanh's beautiful book *The Miracle of Mindfulness* (1975). Thich Nhất Hanh, a Buddhist monk from Vietnam, is recognized as one of the best teachers of mindfulness to Westerners. His book is accessible, engaging, and written with kindness and simple language that won't scare you away.

MEDITATION FOR MANIACS

Are you a person who always has something to do? Chances are that this describes you, or you wouldn't be reading a book about stress management. Life is demanding, pulling you in all different directions. There is always something to buy, to do, to see, to figure out, or to fix. The demands on your attention are never ending, starting with the alarm clock in the morning and ending with the late-night news and its dire warnings of the latest health threat or severe storm somewhere across the planet. You, like most people, probably feel like a maniac at least some of the time, rushing about in your head, your car, and your home to maintain some control over what seems like relentless chaos.

It's vital to your physical, emotional, and psychological health to break the spiral of intensity. You can learn to stop the madness for a few minutes and then dive right back in, refreshed and better able to cope.

One excellent way to do this is to use the three-breath technique. You can do this anytime, anywhere. All you have to do is recognize the signs of stress. As soon as you start to feel overwhelmed, stop for a minute. Say to yourself, *I need a break*. Then take it. Take three breaths with your full attention on each one. Start by fully exhaling, and then calmly, carefully observe the next breath coming in. Feel it expanding inside you, and think to yourself, *Thank you*. Hold the breath for an instant, and then let it out slowly, thinking to yourself, *Let go*. Repeat this twice more. Don't cheat yourself. You have time to do this carefully, slowly, and mindfully. Just give yourself one minute to reconnect with the miracle of your breathing, and then get back to work. If you practice this every day, you'll notice a shift in the way you perceive stress, from something that just keeps happening to you to something you can observe with detachment.

You can find many other short meditation techniques in *The Three-Minute Meditator* by David Harp and Nina Feldman (1996). This book has a wonderful introduction to the art and science of meditation and is full of simple ways to bring meditation into your everyday life.

MINDFUL WALKING

I can't write about meditation, mindfulness, and flow without mentioning my favorite type of meditation: mindful walking. This is simply the act of taking a very slow walk during which you pay close attention to everything that happens. This is a nice thing to do in your neighborhood, in your yard, or in a natural area near where you work. Start by coordinating your breath with your steps. Take a step as you inhale, take a step as you exhale. Continue this for a while, noticing how each foot touches the ground, how your chest expands, whether or not it feels awkward to be walking so slowly. Gradually, turn your attention to your surroundings. It's amazing to discover how many details you've been missing.

If you like mindful walking, you might enjoy tai chi, qi gong, or yoga. Each of these practices involves intense awareness of the body in space, close attention to how you're moving, and coordination with the breath. Each is different, and which you choose may just be a matter of taste. There are classes in each of these at community centers, colleges, and gyms all over the country.

Conclusion

In this chapter, we explored two vital skills for stress management: accessing flow and developing mindfulness. Both of these can be part of your everyday life, giving you a deeper sense of meaning and more potential for happiness and satisfaction in each day.

5

Use Food as Your Medicine

There are profound and intimate connections between diet and stress. The relationship runs both ways: less-than-optimal nutrition can make you more susceptible to stress, and stress can affect your ability to choose healthy food, digest it, and absorb nutrients. In this chapter, you will learn how modern life has changed the way people feel and behave around food; how stress affects what, when, and how you eat; how poor diet can contribute to stress; and how you can use food to manage stress.

Eating in the Modern World

Food is something most people take for granted. You eat several times a day, every day, making food at least as important to your health as any medications you might be taking. Food is essential to life, but it's also fraught with emotional and social baggage. Because our culture values physical appearance, many people spend their lives trying to meet an aesthetic ideal that isn't realistic for the average person. At the same time, you're presented with more and more access to fatty, high-sodium, nutrient-poor food. The mixed messages from advertising and entertainment can create a lot of stress. On the one hand, you're supposed to be thin and fit, but on the other, you're encouraged to eat processed foods and fast food. The indoctrination begins in childhood. During the television shows that U.S. children watch the most, up to 83 percent of the foods advertised are snacks, fast foods, and sweets (Harrison and Marske 2005). Meanwhile, over 16 percent of children and over 65 percent of adults in the United States are overweight or obese (Hedley et al. 2004). Both overweight and obesity are risk factors for a host of diseases, including cardiovascular disease, the number one killer of men and women every year.

FOOD IN FAST-FORWARD

The time pressures of jobs, child care, home management, and all the other requirements of everyday life make it very appealing to simply pull a box out of the freezer, pop it in the microwave, and call it dinner. In the short run, this may seem like a good way to save time and reduce stress. There are several problems with this approach, however. One is that processed foods don't contain the variety of nutrients that your body needs over the long term. These foods appeal to your most basic desires—for sweetness, fattiness, and saltiness. Unfortunately, those sensations come paired with high levels of sugars and other concentrated sweeteners, sodium, and *trans fats*, chemically altered fats that have a longer shelf life but are harmful to human cells (Lopez-Garcia et al. 2005; Oh et al. 2005). When, for the sake of convenience, you sacrifice the daily rituals of buying, preparing, and slowly and consciously eating food, you miss out on the potential social, emotional, and physical advantages of eating while relaxed.

In addition to consuming more convenience foods at home, Americans are eating the majority of our meals outside the home and spending almost half our food budgets on restaurant meals (Young and Nestle 2002). Eating on the run is in itself stressful, and it compromises digestion and the absorption of nutrients. When you're under stress, food stays in your stomach longer, stimulating more acid production and creating more wear and tear on your system. Stress also makes the muscles of your intestines more active, and this can cause symptoms like cramping, diarrhea, and, in some people, constipation (Mayer 2000). Furthermore, stress hormones can disrupt the delicate layer of cells along the intestine, making them less efficient at digestion and absorption (Santos and Perdue 2000).

FOOD IN LARGE QUANTITIES

Fast food has been getting a lot of bad press lately, and rightly so. This food is extremely high in unhealthy fats, calories, and sodium. Portion sizes at fast-food restaurants are two to five times bigger now than they were twenty years ago (Ledikwe, Ello-Martin, and Rolls 2005), resulting in staggering increases in the calorie counts of the typical fast-food meal. The increase in portion size hasn't been occurring only at restaurants, however. In the last decade, the average portion size for meals eaten at home has also dramatically increased. This amounts to a tremendous increase in the average daily intake of calories and is surely a major contributor to the obesity epidemic.

FOOD ANXIETY

The news media frequently present reasons to be afraid of food, from mad cow disease to salmonella contamination to pesticide residues on produce. Often, the reports are unfounded, rely on inadequate research, or exaggerate a minor risk. Yet people respond with fear and confusion, experiencing even more of the stress already inherent in modern life. The Internet has intensified this effect, because news, rumor, and opinion can all seem equally credible and spread like wildfire. It's important to keep food scares in perspective. For the most part, our food supply is safe. The best protection is to eat a wide variety of foods in their most natural form.

Exercise: What Kind of Eater Are You?

This exercise will reveal how stress and eating are related for you. Rate how often each of these things happens in your life. Use the following scale:

never	1
seldom	2
sometimes	3
usually	4
all the time	5

1. I tend to eat more when I feel anxious _____

2. I try to avoid foods that are high in fat _____

3. I never eat meat or poultry _____

4. I eat very little during the day but find myself making up for it at night _____

5. I eat more when I'm alone than when I'm with other people _____

6. I tend to eat when I feel sad _____

7. If I've had a bad day at work, I tend to eat more for dinner _____

8. There are certain foods that I love but won't eat because they're fattening or unhealthy _____

9. When I get frustrated, I eat more _____

10. I have trouble eating only one cookie _____

11. I feel embarrassed after I eat certain foods ____

12. When I'm anxious, I eat a lot of food without even realizing it ____

13. I am on a diet ____

14. When I'm upset, certain foods make me feel better ____

Add up your scores for items 2, 3, 5, 8, 10, 11, and 13. This is your restrictive eating score. Now, add up your scores for items 1, 4, 6, 7, 9, 12, and 14. This is your emotional eating score.

If your emotional eating score is 24 or higher, you may be using food to soothe yourself when you're feeling stressed. This type of eating can be part of a dangerous cycle, because emotional eaters tend to eat unhealthy comfort foods at times of stress, increasing the body's level of stress. You can read more about emotional eating in Eating as a Coping Mechanism and in the rest of this chapter.

If your restrictive eating score is 24 or higher, you may be creating more stress in your life by placing difficult restrictions on your eating behavior. You may be someone who diets frequently and avoids entire food groups, thus depriving yourself of vital nutrients. The psychological impact of rigid or restrictive eating patterns is big—it sets you up for bingeing, stress-related eating, and weight fluctuations. These things only make your life more stressful. See Dieting Is Stressful (and Ineffective) and the rest of this chapter for healthier ways to eat and keep your weight under control.

How Stress Affects Your Diet

Stress can have a powerful effect on appetite and food cravings. As you learned in the introduction, stress is an interaction between you and the environment. Whenever you begin to feel overwhelmed, your whole system reacts by mounting a stress response.

EATING AS A COPING MECHANISM

When you're stressed, your nutritional needs change. Yet this is when most people shift into emergency eating mode. Rushing, eating fast food, eating processed foods, eating standing up or in front of the television: all these habits only make stress more harmful to the body and mind.

Any type of stress—acute or chronic, real or imagined—triggers a response from the nervous and endocrine systems. This response involves many chemicals that act on the brain and the rest of the body to keep you ready to meet a threat. On the surface, it would seem that a constant state of stress arousal would decrease your appetite, and in many people, it does. Yet, as Robert Sapolsky (2004) points out, over two-thirds of people who report feeling stressed also report that they tend to overeat in the face of stress. The gist of his and others' research is that isolated acute stressors may temporarily reduce appetite, but the hormonal changes that occur in the recovery phase tend to stimulate increases in eating. And when your day is dotted by one worry, hassle, or problem after another, you may be spending most of your time in recovery mode, with its attendant elevations in blood cortisol levels.

Some stress-related overeating is simply a habitually pleasant activity. Consider the psychological and emotional reasons you might turn to food when you're feeling overwhelmed. In our society, food is readily available, it's very tasty, and it's cheap. It provides an experience of immediate gratification. Eating is a social endeavor, a pleasure we can share with family, friends, and coworkers. Sharing food and drinking high-calorie beverages like beer are pleasant activities that provide relief from the daily grind. Not surprisingly, body weight tends to increase as work stress gets worse (Kouvonen et al. 2005).

THE STRESS RESPONSE REDUX

In addition to the psychological and social reasons to overeat as a response to stress, there are powerful stress-related biochemical processes that influence eating. One of the chemicals in the brain involved in the stress response is *corticotropin releasing factor* (CRF). It's made in the *hypothalamus,* a small, almond-sized structure deep in the brain that controls primitive, essential functions such as sleep and feeding behavior. Any stressor, whether internal or external, produces an increase in CRF levels in the brain and throughout the body. CRF initiates the rest of the stress response, mostly by stimulating the adrenal glands to secrete their stress hormones, including cortisol. Cortisol affects the function of many different organs in the body, including fat cells and the brain, affecting how much you eat, what you eat, how much fat you store, and where that fat is stored. It's a fascinating story, one scientists are only beginning to put together based on extensive research with rats and human beings.

Stress Makes You Eat More

In the recovery phase of chronic stress, cortisol works to protect the body during a long-term challenge by increasing fat storage. It does this by stimulating a desire for pleasurable activity—including eating (Dallman et al. 2004). This makes sense when you think about human beings living anywhere but in an affluent, developed country. Under conditions of chronic stress, these people would want to keep their strength up by eating more. In most societies and in most periods of human history, food has been scarce. It's only recently that we've become able to pick and choose abundant quantities of highly caloric food. So, here and now, in twenty-first-century America, chronic stress tends to trigger appetite, and food is everywhere. This appears to be a major contributor to rising levels of overweight and obesity. But this is only part of the story.

Stress Makes You Crave Sugar and Fat

Chronic stress seems to affect not only how much you eat, but what you choose to eat. Cortisol and the emotional effects of stress tend to increase the desire for foods that are sweet and high in fat (Epel et al. 2001). Cortisol, when injected into an animal or human being, acts on the hypothalamus to increase the appetite for food that is high in fat or sugar. This is especially true among people who find emotional soothing through eating (Oliver, Wardle, and Gibson 2000). Sweet, fatty foods can induce a release of the brain's natural *opiates*, molecules that decrease pain and create euphoria. This momentary rise in brain opioids can actually create addiction, and withdrawal can occur if the supply of sugar is cut off (Levine, Kotz, and Gosnell 2003).

Stress Directs Fat Storage to the Abdomen

High levels of cortisol cause more fat to be stored in the fat cells of the abdomen. This fat is *visceral fat*, and it is responsible for the "apple" shape that is more dangerous to health than body shapes in which fat is distributed more evenly over the body. Visceral fat is a very real danger to cardiovascular health because of its effects on blood sugar and blood cholesterol. People with large amounts of visceral fat are at higher risk of heart disease, type 2 diabetes, high blood pressure, and premature death. Visceral fat is involved in a high level of metabolic activity that releases *triglycerides* (fatty acids) into the blood and creates insulin resistance, a symptom of type 2 diabetes that results in high blood sugar levels (Goldbacher, Matthews, and Salomon 2005).

A quick way to determine your degree of visceral fat is to calculate your *waist-hip ratio* (WHR), the circumference of your waist divided by the circumference of your hips. A WHR of 0.8 or lower is considered healthy for females; for males, a ratio of 1.0 or lower is desirable. If your ratio is higher than is considered healthy, it's likely that the way fat is distributed in your body is determined in part by your levels of stress. Surprisingly, a high WHR poses many health risks even in people who are not overweight or obese. Elissa Epel and her colleagues (2000) found that an elevated WHR in lean women may be even more dangerous than a high WHR in overweight women, because the lean women had higher cortisol levels in response to stressful events, and they were less likely to adapt to repeated stresses in a laboratory study.

Visceral fat is highly sensitive to cortisol levels, more so than fat located elsewhere. In studies of men experiencing stress at their jobs, the amount of cortisol released with each stressful period throughout the day was greater in men who had more visceral fat than in men who had less (Rosmond, Dallman, and Björntorp 1998). Fat in the abdomen has enzymes that activate cortisol. So visceral fat has a role in perpetuating the chronic stress state—a state that includes immune suppression, poor absorption of nutrients, and increased risk of cardiovascular disease. Visceral fat is also associated with higher levels of cardiovascular reactivity, or elevations in blood pressure and heart rate in response to stress. Goldbacher, Matthews, and Salomon (2005), in a study of 210 adolescents, found that those with higher WHRs had greater elevations in blood pressure during a series of stressful tasks when compared to adolescents with lower WHRs.

Interestingly, visceral fat may act on the brain to suppress the discomfort associated with chronic stress. The specific way that visceral fat interacts with the brain is not clear, but it appears that visceral fat releases a substance (as yet unidentified) that enhances mood even during stress (Dallman et al. 2004).

What kinds of food tend to create abdominal fat? Foods high in carbohydrate and fat, like pastries and ice cream, which tend to be used as comfort food. Eating large amounts of this type of food can have immediate effects on brain chemistry by increasing tryptophan and serotonin levels. *Serotonin* is an important mood-altering neurotransmitter. (In most people with major depression, serotonin levels are abnormally low; abnormal serotonin levels are also present in many people with high levels of anxiety.) *Tryptophan* is the most important chemical building block of serotonin. Eating more high-carbohydrate, high-fat foods makes it more likely that your belly will work to calm your frazzled brain. In this way, you're biochemically rewarded for eating comfort foods and maintaining visceral fat. Indeed, for some people, overeating is an unconscious but real attempt to increase abdominal fat stores because these cells interact with the brain to suppress stress responses and improve mood. The cost of this mood elevation is very high, however, and there are other ways to accomplish this, including taking a thirty-minute walk.

How Poor Diet Can Contribute to Stress

Clearly, stress influences what foods you choose, what your body does with those foods, and how that affects your health. But the equation works the other way, too: your diet can affect your stress levels.

NUTRITIONAL DEFICIENCIES CONTRIBUTE TO STRESS

It may seem ironic in the midst of an obesity epidemic to say that nutritional deficiencies are making people more vulnerable to stress, yet it's true. Whether you eat too much or are dieting to lose weight, your intake of vital nutrients probably isn't adequate for long-term health. This has everything to do with *processed food*, food that has been altered to be more palatable (sweeter or saltier), to be quicker or easier to prepare, or to last longer on the shelf. Processing many types of food, especially whole grains, strips it of its nutrients. Most people's diets are deficient in several nutrients—including zinc, vitamin D, and magnesium—that are important for countering the effects of stress.

In a paper summarizing a survey of over 15,000 American adults, Ashima Kant (2000) of Queens College in New York reported that on average, 31 percent of the calories consumed every day come from energy-dense, nutrient-poor (EDNP) foods. Examples of EDNP foods include visible fat, sweeteners, desserts, and salty snacks like potato chips. Kant also reported that people tend to eat these foods in place of fruits, vegetables, and whole grains, resulting in deficiencies of vitamins and other important nutrients. Basically, as the proportion of EDNP foods goes up in a person's diet, blood levels of important nutrients such as folate, vitamin B_{12}, vitamin C, and beta-carotene go down. In addition, serum levels of HDL (the good cholesterol) also go down as consumption of EDNP foods goes up.

Comfort foods tend to be EDNP foods, and many people eat more of them in response to stress. We have the makings of a vicious cycle here, where inadequate nutrition is both a trigger and a consequence of stress, leading to higher rates of overweight, obesity, and chronic disease.

DIETING IS STRESSFUL (AND INEFFECTIVE)

When people are on a weight-loss diet or other restricted eating regimen, they're much more likely to overeat in response to stress and distressing emotions (Oliver, Wardle, and Gibson 2000). Fascinating new research in this area, published by Mary Boggiano and her colleagues (2005), suggests that dieting is a major trigger of overeating in the face of stress. People who are dieting have smaller amounts of natural opioids, the molecules of pleasure in the brain. The brain compensates by becoming more receptive to even small amounts of natural (or synthetic) opioids. A single cookie or other treat causes a release of these substances in the brain, creating a huge craving that may only be satisfied by a binge. In the pleasure-starved brain, a small amount of relief triggers a strong desire for more. In her experiments with dieting and nondieting rats, Boggiano found that neither stress alone nor dieting alone was enough to trigger binge eating, but a stressor on top of a history of intermittent dieting was enough to bring on a bout of overeating—but only if the rats were given access to highly palatable (read "comfort") food.

This can be translated into human experience quite easily. Imagine you've been on a diet for a week or two, closely watching calories and fat and avoiding foods you really enjoy. Then you have a major upset at work. On your way home, you allow yourself a cookie. Soon, you find yourself at the grocery store, buying more cookies and maybe a quart of ice cream to go with them. Sound familiar?

The upshot of the research on stress and dieting is that to manage weight and stress, restrictive diets may not be such a good idea. In fact, the very act of dieting may make stress worse. Judy McLean, Susan Barr, and Jerilynn Prior (2001) at the University of British Columbia found that young women who were dieting had elevated cortisol levels when compared to similar young women who were not dieting.

OVEREATING IS STRESSFUL

Eating, in and of itself, tends to stimulate the release of cortisol. This effect is greater in women with abdominal obesity than in those who are obese but have fat distributed evenly

(Vicennati et al. 2002). After a large meal, the stomach is distended by food. The body responds to this by increasing blood pressure and heart rate, classic signs of a stress response (Rossi et al. 1998). This is a normal response, but it can become problematic when you eat frequently, and usually eat beyond the point of being satisfied. Many people eat too quickly, overeating before they realize they've had enough. This enhances the stress response that happens after eating. Frequent snacking, especially if the snacks are large, keeps the body in a continually stressed state (Sies, Stahl, and Sevanian 2005).

Every time you eat, your blood becomes flooded with sugars, amino acids, and fats from the food you've consumed. Foods high in fats tend to create large increases in the concentration of fat in the blood, making it thicker and more susceptible to clotting. Mental stress tends to enhance this effect, possibly making fatty foods more dangerous shortly after they're eaten (Le Fur et al. 1999). As portion sizes and caloric density increase, so does the metabolic burden on your body, creating more wear and tear.

One way to counteract these effects is to eat more slowly and deliberately, and to focus on the bodily sensations of chewing, swallowing, and sensing the food in the stomach. The mindful eating exercise in the next section will help you learn to avoid eating too much too quickly.

Using Food to Manage Stress

Food can be one of your best stress management tools, if you use it wisely. It's okay to eat for comfort, as long as you're choosing foods that create calm nourishment for your body. The comfort level goes up even more if you take the time to prepare the food yourself and serve it simply and beautifully. Eating healthful food slowly and mindfully, in the presence of people you care about, is one of life's great pleasures. Yes, it takes a little more time to eat this way, but the rewards are priceless.

WHAT TO EAT

Developing a nutritional plan for stress management is a highly individualized process that requires attention and a willingness to experiment. However, it's safe to say that you will benefit from balancing your diet, eating lots of vegetables, and choosing foods in their natural state. Certain nutrients can be helpful in managing stress. Some of these nutrients are depleted by chronic stress, and some help make your body and mind more resilient. Be sure to let your doctor know if you significantly change your nutritional plan, especially if you add supplements to your diet. They may interact with prescription medications in important and unpredictable ways.

Balance Your Diet for Optimal Brain Chemistry

The first thing to consider is the balance of macronutrients you consume each day. Is your diet loaded with simple carbohydrates, manufactured fats, or processed meats? These foods tend to increase the effects of stress on the body. Start by balancing the amounts of protein, carbohydrate, and fat in your diet. You've undoubtedly heard a lot recently about the ideal proportions of these three macronutrients. But what does this have to do with stress? It's all about brain chemistry.

Your brain communicates with itself and the rest of your body with electrical impulses and neurotransmitters, including dopamine, norepinephrine, and serotonin. Some of your food cravings are actually your body trying to balance the chemistry of your brain. When you become depleted in certain nutrients, your neurotransmitters can become unbalanced. Some of the commonest mental illnesses, including depression and anxiety, involve abnormal levels of neurotransmitters. Many of the prescription drugs used to treat these illnesses work by adjusting neurotransmitter levels in the brain.

PROTEIN. Neurotransmitters are made by the body from *amino acids*, the breakdown products of protein. So your body requires adequate amounts of quality protein to maintain good brain function. Protein should come in the form of lean meats and fish, with an emphasis on fish because it also provides the best kind of fats for fighting stress. Other good sources of protein include nonfat or low-fat cottage cheese and yogurt, eggs, lentils, and kidney beans. If you're a vegetarian, it also might be helpful to supplement your diet with whey protein, because it's nutritionally complete, providing all the essential amino acids your body needs.

FATS. You also need a steady flow of good fats (such as fish oil), because they're used by the brain to transform amino acids into neurotransmitters. Avoid trans fats and other factory-made fats in favor of simple, pure olive oil and canola oil. Read the label on the next packaged food you think of buying. If it includes any kind of fat that's partially hydrogenated, you will do better to avoid eating it.

CARBOHYDRATES. Like protein and fats, carbohydrates influence the levels of neurotransmitters in your brain. As blood levels of tryptophan go up or down in relation to other amino acids, your brain makes more or less serotonin. The body absorbs the most tryptophan from a meal or snack that is high in carbohydrates and low in protein (Fernstrom and Fernstrom 1995). This results in an increase in serotonin levels in the brain, which may lead you to crave this type of food as a form of self-medication when you are anxious or feeling negative emotions (Yanovski 2003). This is okay as long as these cravings are relieved by favoring *complex carbohydrates* (those found in whole-grain foods, fruits, and vegetables) over *simple carbohydrates* (the sugars found in juice, candy, and pastries). Eating simple carbohydrates may produce an exaggerated opiate response in the brain (Levine, Kotz, and Gosnell 2003) and a large insulin response from the pancreas (Oettlé, Emmett, and Heaton 1987), both of which subject your body to wear and tear and a deterioration in mood as well as weight gain.

VITAMINS AND MINERALS. Another important nutrient you need to care for your brain is vitamin C, which is also used to make neurotransmitters. Other nutrients that tend to be depleted when you're under chronic stress are the B vitamins and magnesium.

Eat Your Vegetables

Vegetables are probably the most neglected and most beneficial foods available to us. There is no substitute, no supplement that can replace what they provide. One of the best things you can do for yourself is to fall in love with three or four different vegetables and eat them regularly. Here's a short list, adapted from a review article by Johanna Lampe (1999), of what vegetables can do for you:

- supply your body with *antioxidants*, nutrients that counteract the wear and tear of daily life—and stress

- stimulate the immune system

- help prevent the formation of harmful blood clots

- keep cholesterol metabolism in a healthy range

- fight infections

- keep blood pressure in check

Essentially, by eating more vegetables, you can help your body counteract the effects of stress. The U.S. Department of Health and Human Services and the U.S. Department of Agriculture (2005) jointly recommend that everyone eat at least two and a half cups of vegetables every day. Most people don't come close to this level.

Eat Food in Its Natural State

The best way to get the right balance of healthy proteins, carbohydrates, and fats is to eat more food in its natural state and less highly processed food. You can do this easily by avoiding food that comes in boxes on the shelf or in the freezer section of the grocery story. By doing so, you'll also limit your intake of sodium, sugar, and nonnutritive ingredients like preservatives.

HOW TO EAT

In *Art of the Inner Meal* (1999), Donald Altman suggests that the act of eating has long been a focal point of family and spiritual life. Mealtime in most cultures is a time for families and friends to gather and express gratitude for each other and for their food. It's only in the modern era, in the most developed countries, that we can take food for granted. Throughout the course of human history, food has been something we've had to sweat, strive, and—in many cases—fight for. Serving a hot, hearty meal was once the culmination of a long struggle, and only recently have we lost sight of that.

Mindful eating is the act of slowing down and paying attention while eating. This is an excellent practice for breaking some of the connections between eating and stress. Many problems with overeating come from a sense of needing to hurry up and get to the next thing. It's helpful to reconsider eating and make at least one meal every day an opportunity to slow down and take care of yourself. This exercise will boost your appreciation for food in general and vegetables in particular.

Exercise: A Mindful Snack

Start with a visit to your local grocery store or produce market. Find a vegetable or two that you would like to take home and cook and eat. Perhaps you'll choose one that you've eaten many times and one that's new to you. Be picky; choose only pieces that look fresh, smell good, and have good color and texture.

At home, set the intention that you're going to fully appreciate the food you've chosen. This is going to be a healthy snack, and you may be surprised at how easy it is to prepare. Start by washing it and removing any unwanted leaves, stems, or other parts. Notice the color, texture, and smell of the vegetable. Think about where it came from. Imagine the seeds that were planted, the soil the plant grew in, the sunshine and rain that nurtured it. Try to visualize all the people involved in cultivating and harvesting this food that is now in your kitchen. Consider giving thanks for the miraculous series of events that enable you to be fed every day as easily and readily as you are.

Cook the vegetable carefully, being sure not to overcook it. You can steam it or microwave it. It's done perfectly when the color has peaked in intensity and the texture has become soft enough to chew but not mushy. Choose a nice plate or bowl, and pay attention as you serve. Are you going to put butter on it? Salt? Perhaps it's worthy of a taste before you add anything. You might discover that you like the taste of this food in its basic form.

Now, sit down at the table, with no distractions—no magazine or television. Before you take your first bite, again notice the texture, color, and smell of the vegetable, and see how cooking changes it. Realize that you're about to take a dose of the earth's best medicine, and your body will benefit from just this little bit. Taking your first bite, put down your fork, and give yourself a chance to taste the food. Chew it thoroughly, at least thirty times, before you swallow it. As it goes down, pay attention to how you feel when the food gets to your stomach.

As you continue to eat, try to make every bite as mindful as the first. This may take some practice and patience, but it is well worth it. You will probably notice that you feel satisfied by the time you finish eating this snack. It might be unusual for you to feel satisfied after eating so little food, but this time you've given your body time to register the fact that you're eating before you've eaten too much.

After you've finished, take a moment to reflect on how your body feels. Are you relaxed? Have you experienced pleasure? Take a minute or two and record your impressions in your notebook. Think about trying this exercise once a day for a week, just to see if your appreciation for vegetables, food in general, and the act of eating increases.

Conclusion

In this chapter, we looked at some of the connections between stress, food, and eating. It's a big, complex subject that touches on many aspects of human experience and is connected to deep emotional and spiritual needs. With a better understanding of the connections between food, mood, and stress, and with an intention to use food more mindfully, you'll be taking the first steps toward a better relationship with food, and better health overall.

Get Into Your Body

Movement, especially rhythmic movement, begins long before you're born. In the womb, your heart beat to its own rhythm, independent of your mother's. As soon as you had arms and legs, they were moving—waving, thrusting, swaying in the amniotic fluid day and night. These movements help developing muscles and nerves grow and make connections in preparation for a lifetime of motion. Your chest started moving in and out as you breathed the fluid that surrounded you, bathing your lungs with moisture and nourishment to grow strong and flexible. You grew to the soothing, rhythmic sound and movement of your mother's heartbeat and breathing. Long before you made your entry into this world of light, sound, taste, and touch, you spent months learning to move your body and responding to the body's rhythms.

How Moving Your Body Creates Calm

In the introduction to this book, you learned that the stress response involves a lot of physiological activation; that's why it's called fight or flight. The body is prepared to run away or stand and fight. All systems are "go" during an acute stress response— and, to a lesser degree, in the chronic stress state as well. Keeping your system in a continual state of readiness takes vital resources and energy away from repairing worn-out tissues, fighting infection, growing new cells, digesting and absorbing food, and other life-sustaining activities.

So, how do you shift into a more relaxed state and give your body a break? One answer is: Move it. Think of gazelles that have to run from a predator. They sense the lion and the imminent danger it poses. Do they stand around and obsess about it? Do they make mental lists of what to do and pace around wondering where to start? Do they worry about what the other gazelles will think if they start running willy-nilly to get away? No, of course not. They feel the fear and they run away as fast as they can. They discharge the anxiety with intense physical exertion that, for most of them, saves their lives. Interestingly, that burst of physical activity also helps discharge the extreme stimulation of the stress response, allowing them to go back to placidly chewing grass after the threat has passed.

What can we learn from this? First of all, the stress response is a true physical state that, in modern society, usually comes from threats you think of, not from immediate threats to your physical safety or well-being. You can cope with these stressors using your mind, and many of the solutions in this book help with that. Also, you need to relieve the physical tension that goes along with chronic stress, or it will build and create symptoms like backache, muscle aches and pains, and frequent injuries.

One of the major consequences of chronic stress is insomnia. There is a crisis of sleeplessness in this country, and it's leading to higher rates of depression and anxiety, more auto accidents, and a host of other physical and psychological problems. Regular exercise promotes healthy sleep patterns and can be an effective way to manage insomnia.

What Does Exercise Do?

When I talk about the health benefits of exercise, I mean *aerobic* exercise, the kind that gets your heart pumping and your blood flowing—things like walking, dancing, running, and bicycling. Other forms of exercise, especially weight training and yoga, have tremendous health benefits as well, but my goal is to encourage you to consider increasing the amount of time you're actually up on your feet, moving rhythmically and feeling the surge of well-being and vitality that aerobic exercise provides.

Is part of your stress due to concerns about your health? Do you worry about dying of heart disease, cancer, or another chronic, incurable disease? If so, exercise may be part of the solution to your health-related anxieties. The evidence is overwhelming: regular physical exercise lowers your risk of dying prematurely. It also lowers your risk of suffering debilitating symptoms due to heart disease, stroke, and cancer (Blair, Cheng, and Holder 2001). Yet 75 percent of Americans do not engage in regular physical exercise, and over 30 percent are completely sedentary. Of the three most common lifestyle-based killers in America today, number two is poor nutrition and lack of exercise, which add up to overweight and obesity (Centers for Disease Control 2003). So, if you get moving, you not only get the direct stress-relieving benefits of regular physical activity, you also protect yourself from chronic disease and probably live a longer, more vital life.

EXERCISE AND PHYSICAL HEALTH

During and after a bout of moderate to intense exercise, the immune and endocrine systems get fired up (Pederson and Hoffman-Goetz 2000). There is an increase in inflammatory markers, and the blood profile looks similar to that of an acute infection. Antibodies are released, and white blood cells are mobilized. Adrenaline gets released, and this seems to affect the immune system. Although a bout of exercise stimulates the immune system in several ways, these effects are usually short-lived. In fact, people who engage in regular exercise tend to have lower levels of inflammation than similar adults who don't exercise (Abramson and Vaccarino 2002). Inflammation is the underlying problem in many chronic ailments, including *atherosclerosis* (arterial plaque that leads to heart attacks and strokes) and some forms of arthritis. Long-term reduction in inflammation may be one way that exercise protects against disease.

In addition to immune changes, there are many hormonal responses to exercise. Growth hormone levels increase (Kanaley et al. 2001), which makes sense because a bout of intense exercise often results in microdamage to muscle tissue. Growth hormone helps these tissues repair themselves and grow stronger. This is one way that regular exercise can counter the effects of chronic stress, which tends to result in lowered levels of growth hormone over time (Sapolsky 2004). Pleasure hormones like beta-endorphin are released in the brain, creating the euphoria most people feel during and after exercise. Testosterone levels also rise in men and women after moderate to intense exercise. In the immediate phase, exercise is actually a stressor; it calls upon the body to mount a response similar to fight or flight, but it does so in a healthy way.

In their landmark 1989 study of over 12,000 adults, Steven Blair and his colleagues presented solid evidence of the protective effects of physical fitness against premature death. They found that lack of physical activity and fitness greatly increases your risk of dying from a variety of causes, regardless of whether you smoke, have high blood pressure or cholesterol, or have parents who died of heart disease. JoAnn Manson and her colleagues (1999) examined life histories of over 72,000 women, looking at exercise levels and the incidence of disease and death, and found that walking was just as effective as more vigorous forms of exercise in staving off heart disease and death. They also found that it's never too late to start exercising. Women who started exercising in middle age reaped big benefits compared to women who remained sedentary. In order to dramatically boost your chances of living longer and being healthier, you only have to take a brisk thirty- to sixty-minute walk every day. That's all.

EXERCISE AND MOOD

Regular physical activity improves mood, even for people with major depression (Dimeo et al. 2001). This is also true for the very old; regular exercise enhances the ability to continue performing the tasks of daily living and promotes positive moods and a sense of meaning in life (Kahana et al. 2002). Exercise has a strong effect on self-esteem.

Physical fitness seems to function as a type of buffer, or protective factor, between stressful life events and their possible negative impact on physical health (Roth and Holmes 1985). In a study of mice that exercised regularly compared to sedentary mice, Susanne Droste and her colleagues (2003) found that the exercising mice had relatively lower levels of stress hormones in response to psychological stressors such as being introduced to a strange environment. In a study of people with high blood pressure, Anastasia Georgiades and her colleagues (2000) found that people who had exercised regularly for six months fared much better than people who hadn't exercised when confronted with a psychological stressor in the laboratory. The exercisers had lower blood pressure and heart rate before, during, and after the stressor, compared to the nonexercisers. This is a big benefit in stress management, because one of the ways that stress is harmful is that it amplifies your normal increase in blood pressure and heart rate in response to a difficult situation, putting you at risk for high blood pressure and cardiovascular disease over the long haul. Similar results were seen in a study of adolescent girls in Japan (Nabkasorn et al. 2006). Girls with mild to moderate depression were divided into two groups. One group participated in an exercise program for eight weeks, and the other continued their usual routines. After the eight weeks, the exercisers had significantly lower levels of stress hormones in their urine, and also had lower resting heart rates, reflecting both cardiovascular fitness and reduced effects of stress. The exercisers also had big reductions in their depression symptoms.

Setting Exercise Goals

How much exercise do you need? The short answer is, probably not as much as you thought you did. But really, it depends on your goals. Do you need to lose weight? Do you want to become physically fit at an athletic level? Is there a sport you want to be able to continue well into your older life? Or do you simply want to manage stress and stave off some of the risks of chronic illness? The first thing to do is decide realistically what you want to gain from regular exercise. Then you have to believe that you will gain these things. Then you have to believe that you can do it. If you can't buy in to an exercise program at the level you think you need, you may have to reassess your goals. Maybe all you really want is to be able to take a walk a few days a week to keep your heart and lungs in good working order and enjoy the relaxation of moderate physical activity.

It's also important to regularly reevaluate your goals, because they may change as your fitness level changes. Many people start with walking for relaxation and better health, get stronger, and decide they really want to be runners. That's what happened to me. It wasn't easy to make that transition, and I still backslide into relaxing walking, but for me, the exhilaration of running down a forest trail and sticking with it for a couple of miles simply can't be had any other way. The sheer joy of running is what turns me on, not the long-term health benefits. As long as I'm getting a minimum amount of exercise for health maintenance, everything else is gravy. I also enjoy skiing, and I've found that running has made me a stronger, more confident skier. This motivates me further to increase the intensity of my exercise. Whenever running becomes a chore or feels intimidating, however, I simply allow myself to take it easier and just go for the basics.

HOW HARD AND HOW OFTEN?

One frequent source of confusion about exercise is deciding how hard to work and how often it needs to be done. This is partially determined by your goals, but it helps to understand what really works to bring the benefits of exercise into your life.

Here's what the research shows: If you advise people who are completely sedentary to start exercising, you're going to get the best results if you ask them to perform moderate exercise at a high frequency than if you ask for high-intensity exercise at all or moderate intensity at a low frequency (Perri et al. 2002). When prescribed exercise by doctors and other health care professionals, people tend to do about 60 percent of what they're advised to do. Sixty percent of five to seven days a week means more minutes per week spent exercising than 60 percent of three to five days a week. This is important to keep in mind when you set your own goals for how often you want to exercise.

The other side of the equation is intensity. High-intensity exercise is intimidating to many people. It creates a more dramatic response from the heart and lungs, increases the likelihood of injury, and in the early phases, it's just not as much fun. It's best to start with moderate-intensity exercise and see where that takes you. If you stay at that level indefinitely, you'll still be reaping excellent benefits to your stress levels and overall health.

Another promising bit of research suggests that short sessions of exercise are as effective as long sessions for losing weight and increasing physical fitness. John Jakicic and his colleagues (1999) worked with two groups of overweight women. One group was instructed to exercise five days a week for twenty minutes a day, building up to forty minutes per day, all in one session. The other group was asked to do the same amount of exercise but to break it up into ten-minute segments. Both groups lost weight and got fit, and in the long term, there was no real difference in their weight-loss outcomes. Among women who did short sessions, those who had exercise equipment at home tended to continue their exercise programs longer. This makes sense, because it's easy to jump on a treadmill for ten minutes if it's right there in your house. This study did not measure stress levels, mood, or symptoms of depression, so we can't draw any definite conclusions about short- versus long-session exercise for stress management. However, if being out of shape and overweight is a source of stress for you, anything that helps you lose weight and get fit will probably help you manage the stress in your life more effectively.

Conclusion

One of the best ways to manage stress is to figure out a way to move your body every day. You are a physical being, built for walking, bending, and stretching. This is a natural way for your body and mind to discharge stress and tension. You don't need to be an athlete to get the benefits of physical movement; you only need to remember to walk or dance or do some physical work every day to change your brain chemistry, your nervous system and immune function, and the way your body feels—all for the better.

7

Express Yourself

E veryone has feelings, but not everyone knows how to express feelings in a way that serves them. Ideally, feelings lead to self-expression, which develops your self-awareness and boosts your confidence in your ability to weather challenges and losses. In this chapter, we'll examine how repression of negative emotions like anger and sadness can harm you in body, mind, and spirit. Repression is actually a learned coping mechanism that can be replaced with self-expression, a more natural, healthy way of coping with stress. Disclosure is a form of self-expression that allows you to tell stories about the things that have hurt you. You'll learn how disclosure can work as a stress management tool. I'll discuss therapeutic approaches based on disclosure, including psychotherapy, support groups, and art therapy. Then we'll explore writing and art, two forms of self-expression that allow your emotions to flow naturally. You'll find that you don't need to fear your strong emotions; you only need to recognize them for the transient psychological and physical states they are. Feelings are a source of information and energy you can use to make healthy choices now and in the future.

Repression and Stress

Over one hundred years ago, Sigmund Freud proposed that most mental illness was caused by anxiety, stress, and *repression*, or suppressing of emotions. Freud believed that keeping troublesome memories out of everyday awareness requires energy and effort that, over time, becomes more than the healthy mind can handle. Eventually, these repressed emotions and memories begin to surface, usually in the form of neurotic, anxious behavior. Freud also theorized that suppressed material emerges as physical symptoms. Many illnesses were recognized in Freud's day as *psychosomatic*, or caused by links between anxiety in the brain and the workings of the body.

Many of Freud's theories fell out of favor in the twentieth century, with the rise of other theories about how people behave and what people think. Yet even in the most advanced settings, such as trauma care and cancer treatment, we are constantly reminded that when it comes to preventing and treating illness, what a person thinks and feels is at least as important as what we see on an X-ray or a lab test.

REPRESSION AS A COPING STYLE

Your thoughts, feelings, and memories are a source of stress. Things happen in life that are upsetting, painful, and traumatic. How traumatic these events are depends entirely on your perceptions of them. As upsetting things happen, you find ways to manage your feelings about them. Perhaps you, like most people, sometimes do this by setting your feelings aside and not thinking about them very much. If you do remember, the emotions that go along with the memory are often unpleasant, and you may find yourself wanting to avoid that experience. In Freud's view—and the modern one—it requires a lot of mental effort to not think about things, to store painful memories away, and to not allow yourself to feel anger, grief, and sadness. It really does cause stress. And now researchers are discovering that repression also affects your body through your endocrine and immune systems.

Life presents you with challenges and stressors every day, and you respond by coping. As you learned in chapter 2, you can't always control the amount of stress you're exposed to, but you can choose how you cope with it. Some ways of coping are healthier than others. A repressive, avoidant coping style is one of the less healthy ways. This style involves strategies such as suppressing your feelings, minimizing the importance of distressing events, avoiding situations that might be stressful, refusing to talk about things that bother you, and using television and computer games to hide from how you feel. (This is not to say that everyone who watches television is doing it to numb out, but it's a convenient way to do so when life feels stressful.)

WHAT'S SO BAD ABOUT REPRESSION?

Repression leads to physical, social, and psychological problems. In *Why Zebras Don't Get Ulcers* (2004), Robert Sapolsky discusses the harmful physical effects of emotional suppression. On the surface, it appears that emotional suppression could be a protective way of keeping your cool in a crisis. However, as Sapolsky points out, many people who actively suppress strong emotions in times of stress have sharp increases in their blood pressure, heart rate, muscle tension, and other physically debilitating symptoms when presented with a difficult task or other stressful challenge.

In a 1998 study of women infected with HIV, Luigi Grassi and his colleagues found that those who used a repressive, avoidant coping style had relatively poor immune function, compared to women who used a more active coping style. Optimal immune function is important for all of us, but more so for people with HIV, because the virus attacks immune cells directly. Good immune function is also critical for people with cancer. Janine Giese-Davis and her colleagues

(2004) found that women with breast cancer who had an emotionally repressed coping style had abnormal daily rhythms of the stress hormone cortisol compared to women who were better able to express emotion. Immune function and the progression of cancer growth are intimately connected to fluctuations in cortisol and other stress hormones.

Socially, emotional repression creates a mismatch between what's being said and how it's being said. Body language can speak volumes, and very often, when people are angry or upset, they communicate that emotional state very clearly even as they deny it verbally. Muscle tension, a twitch of the eyelid, clenched fists, facial blushing, and restlessness clearly convey that you're having a strong emotional experience. If you deny these feelings in conversation, you can elicit discomfort and even stress responses in the people you're interacting with. In a 2003 study conducted at Stanford University by Emily Butler and her colleagues, women who suppressed emotions during encounters with other people had measurable increases in blood pressure, a reliable measure of stress—and so did the people they were speaking to. Emotional suppression creates barriers to rapport, intimacy, and the healthy relationships you need in order to thrive.

Storing up your feelings and memories of life's upheavals gives them more power. Suppressed feelings and memories become contorted and force themselves into your awareness in ways that are uncomfortable and hard to manage. They can come to you in dreams or obsessive thoughts. An extreme example is *post-traumatic stress disorder*, a condition marked by the inability to come to terms with traumatic experience, be it a single event or an ongoing situation that exceeds your ability to cope. Up to one-third of people who go through disasters like 9/11 or a hurricane, lose a loved one to death, are victimized by violent crime, or have a major medical catastrophe will go on to develop post-traumatic stress disorder. One of the symptoms of post-traumatic stress disorder is *intrusion*, or unwelcome memories of the trauma.

Healthy Coping Strategies

If emotional suppression is not an optimal way to meet the challenges of stress, then what is? What types of coping are best for your physical, emotional, and social health? There has been a tremendous amount of research in this area, and most of it points to the benefits of active forms of coping, including disclosure and self-expression.

THE BENEFITS OF EXPRESSING EMOTIONS

There are many ways to express emotion, from the artistic to the verbal. What's important is that you feel what you feel and allow yourself to bring your feelings into the world where you can acknowledge them and deal with them. Many people feel intimidated by strong emotion, as if they'll be swept away if they allow it. Boys are taught not to cry when they're upset, and girls are discouraged from displaying anger. Throughout childhood and into our adult lives, we're told that emotion is to be controlled and, in many cases, denied. Many people learn early on that to be accepted by others, they have to maintain their emotions within narrow boundaries.

Emotional constriction isn't healthy for you as an individual or for your relationships with others. Emotions are natural occurrences that involve body, mind, and spirit. They have a trigger, a beginning, a middle, and an end. Unless you're severely stressed, it would be unusual for you to be locked into an emotional state for very long. The natural flow of emotion is like waves on a beach. They arrive, sometimes with great power, and then they disperse. Your job is to allow this to happen so you can make use of the information feelings carry along with them. You can manage stress much more effectively if you learn to allow your feelings to come and go.

ALLOWING NEGATIVE EMOTION TO BE

In *The Gift of Fear* (1997), Gavin de Becker explains that it's actually healthy to feel fear, anxiety, and apprehension at times. How strange that we need to be told this. Yet our culture emphasizes positivity and forward movement. We try to do it all, to live up to unrealistic expectations, and to do it with a smile. After all, we know that stress is bad for our health and we need to find ways to cope with it. Unfortunately, we often mistake skillful stress management with the ability to be satisfied and peaceful all the time. This expectation can often create more stress.

Sadness, anger, frustration, resentment: these are all normal emotional states that must be allowed to come and go. Paradoxically, the more you try to deny your negative emotions, the more powerful they become, and the more stress they cause. Many psychological studies have shown that suppression is completely ineffective. A compelling thought or emotion will persist in its demand for attention until it's given its due. Only then will it lose its potency and fade away.

Twelve years ago, my father died suddenly at the age of fifty-seven. My mother was overcome with grief and anxiety about managing his small printing business and settling his estate. In the weeks after his death, she found herself crying every day, unable to make the phone calls and business decisions that seemed so urgent. She visited her physician, who prescribed antidepressants. Within another few weeks, my mother's grief had subsided, and she felt more capable. But she was numb. For months, she carried on this way, getting things done and feeling very little. Eventually, this numbness began to concern her, so she started working with a therapist. Over time, she realized that she needed to discontinue the medication and take up the grieving process where she had left off. This was a scary decision, but she believed that if she didn't allow herself to feel the loss and fear, she would never be able to move on. In the months that followed, she discontinued her medications, worked with a therapist, and wrote a great deal in her journal. She was sad, lonely, and scared. But eventually these feelings subsided and she found new purpose in her life, and she cultivated connections with friends and family that she hadn't felt a need for while my father was alive. Now, she has remarried, and she lives a vital, happy life that has room for sadness, but also has room for joy and humor.

Exercise: Tracking Negative Emotions

This exercise will help you start to understand your own coping mechanisms and your tolerance for negative emotions. Think of the last time something happened that made you feel angry or frustrated or sad. It needn't be a major trauma, but choose something that made you genuinely upset—perhaps a big disappointment or an argument with someone important to you. The goal is to carefully dissect your reaction to uncover your physical and emotional responses as well as the story you tell yourself when things go wrong.

Now think about how you thought, felt, and behaved in the moments after the feeling began. As you read the following questions, write your responses in your notebook.

1. How and where did the emotion reside in your body? Did you feel your muscles get tense, did your heart rate increase, did you need to pace around, or did you go numb? What did you feel physically, and where in your body did you feel it? If

you call up the memory vividly, you may be able to sense those same physical responses as if the event were happening right now, only less intensely.

2. Now consider what your first impulse was about what to do about the feeling. This is important. Was your first impulse one of escape or approach? That is, did you want to curl up in front of the television with some ice cream, or did you want to call the person and shout it out? How did your mind and thoughts respond to the feelings you were having in your body? Tracking these responses will give you clues to your style of coping.

3. Now take a moment to remember how long the feeling lasted, and how it passed away. Also, take note of whether you felt a sense of completion when the feeling had passed, or if you still felt vaguely (or acutely) dissatisfied.

4. If you've conjured up the memory in a way that brought on a physical response, take a moment now to relax your body and let the memory go. Take in a long, slow breath, focusing on filling your chest and letting go of any tension there and in your shoulders. Next, exhale slowly, saying to yourself, *I am sending this memory back to the past, where it belongs. It's over, and now I can relax.* If you need to, repeat this step a couple of times until you feel comfortable.

5. Finally, jot some notes about whether or not the responses you listed in step 2 were helpful. This requires some frank self-awareness and a willingness to look critically at what you say and do. Did you fly off the handle and berate the person you were angry at? Did you smile and say everything was okay even though it wasn't? Part of healthy self-expression is being able to notice, name, and discuss emotions even when they're uncomfortable.

ACCEPTING NEGATIVE EMOTION

You can learn effective ways to manage emotion, but the first thing you need to do is accept your sadness and anger along with your contentment and joy. You can think of these feelings as signals that there are things you need to pay attention to, and if you do that skillfully, the emotions will flow naturally out of your body, leaving room and energy for the things you care about. Sometimes, the best thing you can do is just allow yourself to feel bad for a while, and see what lessons there are in the feeling. If the feeling is very strong, it's extremely helpful to engage in strenuous physical activity to release the muscle tension and jitteriness.

There is great comfort and wisdom in knowing that you can tolerate a few hours of sadness without falling apart or needing to run away. You're exercising your power as a thinking, feeling being to experience the gamut of human emotion without hiding. As you move through the feeling, you can get to the thoughts and beliefs that lie beneath it, and you come to understand yourself better.

The Benefits of Disclosure and Self-Expression

Disclosure and self-expression provide ways to reduce the stress of constantly suppressing your feelings. Disclosure involves developing coherent stories about problems. In their review of coping styles, Susan Roth and Lawrence Cohen (1986) pointed out that strategies such as disclosure create opportunities to reframe things in a more positive light, to take action, and to feel more in control of situations that are stressful. A study by Anne Fontana and Mary McLaughlin (1998) found that tension reduction and positive reappraisal are associated with less extreme heart rate and blood pressure responses to stressful events.

People find many ways to use self-expression to resolve stress on their own, and some of these strategies are healthier than others. Self-expression can be difficult, so people often use alcohol or other substances to free themselves to say and do things they ordinarily wouldn't do. Sometimes this is fun and harmless, but it often leads to risky behaviors. Stressful occasions lower your defenses and make it more likely that you'll say or do something hurtful to yourself or others. Bottling up feelings only makes them more concentrated. When they're released, they tend to be harder to control. If self-expression can flow more freely during your everyday life, you'll have less material to release at times of stress or under the influence of alcohol or drugs.

It is important to avoid being abusive with your emotions—to not use their power to manipulate or hurt other people. It's possible to allow yourself to feel anger and grief, and even share these feelings with other people without harming them or the relationship. The more you practice this, the better you'll get at it. Over time, you'll learn that emotions, especially strong ones, usually don't last very long. If you allow the emotion to arise, notice it, and pay attention to how it feels and what words go along with it, you can feel safer the next time it comes up.

In the last few years, there has been a surge of interest in the positive effects of writing and talking about painful experiences. Studies have shown that disclosure in one form or another can improve physical symptoms, immune function, and memory. It's also an effective tool for finding and creating meaning in life's ups and downs and forging stronger connections with the people in your life.

IMPROVING PHYSICAL SYMPTOMS AND IMMUNE FUNCTION

In a landmark study published in the *Journal of the American Medical Association* in 1999, Joshua Smyth and his colleagues investigated the possible benefits of writing about stressful events for a group of people with asthma and another with rheumatoid arthritis. People with these conditions were chosen because both diseases involve specific problems with the immune system that create symptoms, and stress is strongly linked with worsening of those symptoms. The participants were divided into three groups: a control group, a group that wrote about a neutral topic, and a group that wrote about a very painful past event. Before the writing exercise, all the participants were tested extensively for disease symptoms, levels of emotional distress, and immune function.

Participants in the active group wrote for twenty minutes a day, four days in a row, about the disturbing event. There was no follow-up counseling or psychotherapy. Disclosure in the form of writing was the only active ingredient in the experiment. Immediately after the four days of writing, all the medical and psychological tests were repeated. The results were astounding.

Patients who wrote about a stressful experience had big changes in every area measured, compared to patients in the control groups. The asthma patients had less difficulty breathing, and the rheumatoid arthritis patients reported significantly less swelling and pain in their joints. The immune systems of the people who did the writing exercise also showed big improvements. These amazing benefits were still present four months later. The researchers concluded that it was the act of disclosure and its positive effects on coping with stress that caused these dramatic changes.

STRENGTHENING MEMORY

It's very common for people under stress to complain that they have trouble remembering things. Memory loss isn't a natural function of aging; it's not necessarily your fate. Most of the memory lapses and problems that people have in middle age are due to stress. Kitty Klein, in *The Writing Cure* (2002), catalogued several studies demonstrating that expressive writing makes working memory work better. Essentially, *working memory* is what allows you to maintain focus and concentration in the face of distractions and interference (which can often take the form of worry and anxiety). It appears that self-expression frees up your mind from worry and allows you to use the power of working memory for the challenges of daily life. This in turn can make life seem less stressful, giving you even more energy to thrive and be creative.

CREATING MEANING

Self-expression through writing or talking can help you create meaning out of painful events. One of the most effective ways to handle a troubling event is to talk about it with friends and family. It's common for people to tell the story over and over again in the immediate aftermath of an event like a death or the loss of a job. As these conversations happen, the stories become more focused, shorter, and more succinct. They get organized and remembered in a way that makes some kind of sense. The situation is no longer overwhelming; there is a coherent story about what happened. In a study of college students at Temple University (Sloan, Marx, and Epstein 2005), researchers found that participants who wrote about the same traumatic experience three times had big reductions in both psychological distress and physical markers of stress.

STRENGTHENING CONNECTIONS TO OTHERS

Processing problems with other people also strengthens interpersonal bonds. People who help each other through hardships grow closer. They learn to trust each other. They develop confidence that others will be present for them when bad things happen in the future. When you are willing and able to express how you feel, you gain many opportunities to get closer to the people in your life.

Disclosure with a Therapist

Disclosure is a key element of psychotherapy, support groups, and art therapy, each of which can be a very effective approach to stress management.

PSYCHOTHERAPY

In psychotherapy, the therapist and client create a one-on-one relationship grounded in trust and healthy boundaries. Over time, the client feels able to reveal feelings and memories to the therapist in words. Depending on the type of therapy, the therapist offers strategies for dealing with these feelings. To a certain extent, which strategy is chosen isn't as important as the safety of the relationship and the power of disclosure. Research into the effectiveness of psychotherapy has shown that for the most part, all types of therapy, from psychodynamic to cognitive behavioral, are equally effective. The important thing is to find a therapist you feel comfortable with.

Many people avoid going to psychotherapy for a variety of reasons, from financial costs to the worry of being labeled mentally ill. But psychotherapy helps, and one of the active ingredients is disclosure. It's also becoming more widely used and less stigmatized as its benefits become known. Most insurance plans cover at least a few weeks of psychotherapy.

SUPPORT GROUPS

Social support is well established as a factor that protects against stress and disease. In support groups, people come together in a controlled environment and talk about themselves. Painful things come up, and they're shared with the group. Thousands of people have participated in groups and have had improvements in their ability to cope with stress, in their physical symptoms, and in their overall quality of life. Disclosure plays an important role in the power of a support group as members work together to create meaningful stories about the challenges they face.

ART THERAPY

Art therapy is a special form of psychotherapy that uses art to express feelings and find solutions to problems. For many people, especially children, this is a good way to get access to feelings that are hard to put into words. Art therapists use drawings, paintings, clay, and other materials to help people express their feelings. Talking about the artwork provides clients an opportunity to explore issues that they might not otherwise be able to recognize and understand.

There is considerable evidence that the mind uses imagery and sensation as the primary mode of learning and remembering. That is, much of what you know and remember is stored in the form of sensory information about how things looked, felt, sounded, smelled, and tasted. It's helpful to have a verbal story as part of the memory, but it's very difficult to remember anything without an image to go along with it.

Creative Self-Expression

Even without a therapist, you can use the power of disclosure very effectively to manage the stress in your life. You can use focused writing, journaling, and art to express what you're feeling and clarify what you're thinking. You don't ever have to share what you create with other people. It's enough to simply take the time to express yourself. There are many ways to do this, and you can keep trying different things until you find what you like best.

Creative self-expression will eventually strengthen your ability to communicate with other people and be more open in your relationships. It's especially important to be able to express anger and sadness, because these emotions seem to do the most harm if they're denied or suppressed.

When you start expressing yourself, feelings will come up, and this can be uncomfortable sometimes. You might wonder why you're doing it. But most likely, you'll soon feel calmer and more optimistic than you did before. The negative emotion passes, and the mind has less work to do keeping it at bay. After a while, as you develop confidence, you'll feel more able to allow the feelings to happen.

You are a creative person simply by virtue of being alive, but you can cultivate your creativity by using your personal experience as raw material. Your thoughts, feelings, perceptions, dreams, ideas, mistakes, and triumphs are rich fodder for growth and worthy of close attention. Expressing them is a great beginning to getting to know yourself better in the here and now, and deciding where you want to go next. After all, the greatest act of creativity is simply creating your own life from moment to moment, day to day. Here are some ideas to get you started.

JOURNALING

Journaling is an ancient practice that goes all the way back to cave paintings. Making a journal fulfills a need to notice, record, and revisit the events in your life and the world you live in. Disclosure is the key; you bring things out onto paper, where they can be processed, reread, and perhaps eventually destroyed. There is no wrong way to journal. If you've taken the time to put pen (or crayon or brush) to paper, you have succeeded in deepening your experience of your life.

Journaling is good practice for the times when you're not actually writing. When you write about something, you have to tune in to it, choose words to describe it, and arrange your narrative. This work gives you the experience of recognizing, acknowledging, and organizing your experience on paper and being successful at it. Continued practice can help you feel more able to acknowledge and organize what you're feeling and thinking in the moment, day by day. You become a more active coper, one who feels more confident that life's ups and downs won't overwhelm you. Journaling can help you develop the sense of mastery that comes with organizing and expressing your inner experience.

VISUAL JOURNALING

Visual journaling involves the use of drawings, collage, abstract imagery, photographs, and other visual elements in your journal pages. For many people, images enrich the journaling process by adding an emotional element to the page. It doesn't require any training in art or any kind of talent. It's like the projects you did in grade school—cutting and pasting, doodling, adding color, and seeing what develops. The benefits of visual journaling are similar to those of art therapy.

Find a blank book with good, thick paper. It may have lines or not, and it can be any size. In my workshops, participants use eight-by-ten-inch hardbound sketchbooks. Some days you may only want to write, and other days you can pull out the markers and glue sticks and let your mind roam free. To get started, simply write different parts of your journal entries in different colored pens. This alone brings the page alive and elicits more emotion. The famous Rorschach test uses color to assess a person's emotional state. Pay attention to the colors you use in your work, and how you feel about them after you're done writing or drawing. This can be helpful information as you get to know yourself and your feeling states better.

The most important tool for visual journaling is your courage and your spirit. Because you're making art that is only for you, you can freely express yourself and dare yourself to make mistakes. Draw a stupid picture, write a clumsy poem, and sketch a deer that ends up looking like a brown Volkswagen. Anything goes. If nobody else ever sees a single page of your journal, your art will be in no way diminished, because you experienced the process of making it. If you keep at it, you'll develop some techniques that will be very pleasing to you. You'll create a few pages that you'll actually want to share with someone because they're so real, or so beautiful, or just so *you*. Over time, you will also reconnect with the part of you that longs to manifest your spirit in the here and now, in the world of the five senses, where it can be held and seen and touched and smelled and learned from, if only by you. That is what art is all about.

STORYTELLING

You can gain perspective on your life by telling the stories of your life to other people. You probably already do this often, when you meet someone new or debrief with your partner at the end of each day. Storytelling can be a special, meaningful activity to share with people you're close to. Here are some ideas for creating a storytelling event.

Set aside an evening to gather with your family or a group of your friends for storytelling. Ask everyone to come prepared to share a personal story. This can be as simple or elaborate as you wish. You can leave it open-ended or have a theme, like favorite travel stories or birth stories. You can ask people to bring photographs or other mementos of the experience they're going to talk about. Create atmosphere with candles, food and drink, or music.

Before the storytelling begins, ask that as each person speaks, everyone else listen with their ears, hearts, and minds, with no interruptions. If children are involved, you may need to set a time limit. Then, simply take turns telling and hearing stories.

Intentional storytelling provides an opportunity for connection, understanding, and self-expression that you simply don't get in everyday life. It's up to you to create moments that allow you and the people you care about to share yourselves fully with one another.

Exercise: Writing About a Stressful Event

You can begin working with disclosure to manage stress by trying a technique similar to the one used in the experiments with people who had asthma and rheumatoid arthritis. This exercise is an effective, easy way to gain mastery over upsets and challenges, and the feelings they bring up.

Commit to doing this exercise over the next four days. Think about when during your day you can find thirty minutes of uninterrupted time to sit quietly and reflect and write.

Early morning might work well, because any emotional stimulation you might feel can dissipate during the rest of the day. Resolve to carry this exercise through to its completion and to pay attention to how it affects you by recording your reactions in your stress notebook.

Here are the steps for each day of writing:

1. Choose a quiet place where you won't be disturbed. If you have to, hang a *Do not disturb* sign on your door. Collect your notebook and writing pen.

2. Take a moment to choose an experience from your past that was distressing. This will be your target experience, the one you'll write about for the next four days. Choose something that was upsetting but not so traumatic that you can't think about it without being overwhelmed. Set the intention that you will allow whatever memories, thoughts, and feelings you have about this event to simply flow from you into your writing.

3. Take five minutes or so to sit quietly and relax your body. Sit in your chair and gaze softly at a spot a couple of feet in front of you. Don't try to focus on anything; let your gaze be soft and unfocused. As an alternative, you may close your eyes.

4. Begin by observing your breath, paying attention to it as you inhale and exhale. Think about allowing your abdomen to fill out as you inhale and to soften as you

exhale. This will make your breath deeper and more relaxing. You may notice that your shoulders slump slightly, your jaw may slacken, and muscle tension in other areas may loosen. Just allow this to happen.

5. After a few minutes, bring the target experience into your mind. Let yourself remember it as fully as you can, allowing the feelings that go along with the memory to come up. If you start to feel overwhelmed, go back to paying attention to your breath until you feel calmer. Then return to the memory where you left off.

6. Note the time. Then, pick up your pen and start to write. Don't edit or cross things out—just keep writing. Let your stream of consciousness come freely to the paper, even if what you're writing makes little sense. Don't worry about incriminating yourself. This is about the process, not the product. You can shred or tear it up when you're done. The important thing is to feel free and unencumbered in your expression of what happened and how you felt.

7. Keep writing for twenty minutes, or until you feel a sense of completion.

At first, you may notice that this exercise brings up anxiety or other uncomfortable feelings. As long as they're not severe, see if you can allow these feelings to arise, notice them, and then allow them to pass away. If this becomes difficult, try doing the exercise focusing on an episode that is less upsetting.

The key to this exercise is to experience bringing an issue to light, allowing it to unfold as a story, being present with the feelings that come along with it, and observing how those feelings have a beginning, a middle, and an end. By doing so, you are practicing active coping and teaching yourself to take a more direct approach to managing stress.

Exercise: Writing a Letter to Someone Who Hurt You

You can also do the previous exercise in the form of a letter to someone who has caused you pain. In most cases, you won't mail the letter. You'll simply give yourself a chance to put your feelings into words as if you were talking to the person. You don't have to worry about the consequences of expressing your feelings, no matter how bitter or petty they may seem. This is a private exercise of disclosure.

To do this, follow the steps above, but before writing, bring the image of the person into your mind, and remember the episode or situation that was painful for you. If it's a long-standing problem, choose a prototypical event to remind you of the source of your feelings about this person. Then complete steps 3 through 7.

Conclusion

In this chapter, we examined the reasons why suppressing your emotions can be harmful to your health and add to the stress in your life. We looked at some exciting research that shows the benefits of disclosure and active coping. You tried some exercises exploring negative emotion and disclosure. Now you can choose a form of emotional expression that you think will work for you, and practice it every day. You can start with the four-day exercise and allow that to lead you into a daily journaling practice. As other events and memories arise, you can do the four-day exercise with them as well. If you persist and be gentle with yourself, you'll discover that you don't have to ignore or deny your fear, sadness, or anger. You can simply allow these emotions to come and go without harming you, just the way feelings like joy, boredom, and contentment tend to do.

Connect with Others

As human beings, we're always connected to other people. In the womb, we are literally connected to our mothers by the umbilical cord. Attachment and bonding begin before we're born, and continue at high intensity during the first two years of life. We learn by observing others. We define ourselves largely by social norms, and by the influence of our parents and role models. We are immersed in relationships, defined by them, nourished by them, and tormented by them.

Relationships can be the best and worst part of human existence, but one thing is certain: their effects are inescapable. We are never free of the influence of other people—this influence is exerted even by the absence of people, as reflected in the health risks of loneliness and isolation. Given the importance of relationships and social connection, it makes sense to learn how they affect stress and health, and to use this understanding to make a better life for yourself and the people you're connected to.

Understanding Your Basic Drive to Connect

Our human need for connection manifests itself as social support, something that is given from one person to another through some type of relationship, be it professional, intimate, or familial. People give social support consciously, with the intention to be helpful. (Of course, it's not always perceived as helpful by the recipient, and this is at the root of many problematic interactions.)

There are four major forms of social support: *emotional support*, or empathy, love, trust, and caring; *instrumental support*, or tangible services; *informational support*, or advice, information, and suggestions; and *appraisal support*, or feedback that helps a person perform self-evaluation (Heaney and Israel 1997). The most extensively studied form of social support is emotional support, but many studies have also focused on informational and instrumental support, sometimes lumping these two together.

The Health Benefits of Social Support

There are probably many ways that social support can help you, but two major pathways have been identified. The first is the direct pathway. Having good social support improves your mood, your sense of well-being, and the function of your body. These direct effects are thought to lead to better health and a longer life. The second way that social support helps is by triggering and fostering better health behaviors. People with good social support tend to take better care of themselves.

Now, in all the research on social support, there are few connections that are definitely causal; that is, you usually can't say which effect causes the other. Perhaps people who tend to be sick more often are also less able to build and maintain social connections, and perhaps being a person who engages in good self-care also means being a person who is good at relationships. The direction of cause and effect isn't always clear in the research, but there are strong, compelling connections between having good relationships and being a healthy, happy person. Decades of research have shown that social support is probably as important a determinant of how long you live as whether or not you smoke, have high blood pressure, or exercise.

DIRECT HEALTH EFFECTS

Daily life can be full of hassles. We now know that daily hassles can create chronic stress responses in the body, and these responses can lead to symptoms and illnesses, including the flu, sore throats, back pain, and headaches (DeLongis, Folkman, and Lazarus 1988). One way that social support seems to work is through its protective effects on the body systems—especially the cardiovascular, endocrine, and immune systems (Uchino, Cacioppo, and Kiecolt-Glaser 1996).

Of the four types, emotional support seems to be the active ingredient in the direct effects of social support. Emotional support serves as a buffer against illness in the presence of stress. It's when you're under stress that you need your social support the most. In their study of married couples, DeLongis, Folkman, and Lazarus found that people with the highest levels of emotional social support and self-esteem had the fewest psychological and physical problems as a result of daily stressful hassles.

In a study of men and women undergoing surgery, Heinz Krohne and Kerstin Slangen (2005) found some interesting differences between men's and women's needs for support. Both men and women were less anxious before surgery if they had high levels of informational support. Women also benefited from high levels of emotional support. In terms of preoperative anxiety, men only benefited from informational support. For both men and women, however, the amount of emotional support available was a strong predictor of how quickly the patient recovered from surgery and got out of the hospital. An interesting possible explanation is that social support has a beneficial effect on immune function and wound healing (Kiecolt-Glaser et al. 1998).

INDIRECT HEALTH EFFECTS

Another way that social support seems to help people be healthier is by encouraging them to take better care of themselves and engage in more health-promoting behaviors. It's almost stereotypical: the wife discourages her husband from eating the sausage hoagie, and the husband encourages the wife to relax more and take better care of herself. There is tremendous research behind this idea, and it appears that practical (instrumental) social support is the most important type for spurring on good health behaviors. It makes sense that having someone around to help you remember to take your medication, to drive you to the doctor's office, or to help you keep track of your appointments is going to help you stay healthy, especially as you age.

The Health Risks of Isolation

Being socially isolated or lonely is very hazardous to your health. People who are lonely tend to have a shorter life span and more disease along the way. There seem to be many reasons for this, some directly physiological and some working through health behavior. The upshot is, if you're lonely or isolated, it would be beneficial to seek some form of human contact that feels good to you. If you have social anxiety, counseling could help you. Being part of a support group, a church congregation, or a club can provide enough social support to have positive effects on mood and health. An alternative is to *give* social support. This is something you can initiate yourself, and it can bring feelings of well-being and accomplishment. It may also be the beginning of new, supportive relationships.

Research has revealed that psychological and emotional factors can have a tremendous impact on immune function and, in turn, how well a person responds to a vaccine. In their study of college students getting flu shots, Sarah Pressman and her colleagues (2005) found that students who reported a high degree of loneliness had higher levels of stress, more negative emotions, poorer sleep, and higher levels of cortisol than students who reported low levels of loneliness. In addition, the lonelier students who also had the smallest social networks showed a significantly poorer response to one of the viruses in the vaccination, reflecting less capable immune function than students who weren't lonely and who had bigger social networks.

Depression and lack of social contact seem to go together, and this combination can place you at risk for alcohol abuse (Peirce et al. 2000). A downward spiral can result if alcohol use or abuse leads you to further avoid social contact, thus making the depression and the need for symptom relief even worse.

Cultivating Good Relationships

Clearly, social support is important in maintaining your health and managing stress. Let's take a look at how you can build relationships that help you cope with stress rather than causing it.

INTIMATE RELATIONSHIPS: IS MARRIAGE HELL?

Marriage is the primary relationship of adults. It's the happy ending to all our fairy tales, and many of our movies and novels and children's cartoons. Once you get married, you are supposed to live happily ever after. Sadly, this doesn't always happen. Around 50 percent of marriages end in divorce. This is not necessarily a bad thing, because under some conditions, a bad marriage can kill you—or at least set you up for a premature death.

The heart seems to be particularly vulnerable to the dangers of marital strain. Women who had previously had a heart attack were followed for five years, being assessed for the level of conflict and strain in their marriages (Orth-Gomér et al. 2000). Women with high levels of marital strain were almost three times more likely to have had another heart attack or other cardiac emergency than women with low levels of marital conflict, even aside from health behaviors and disease severity. In another study, James Coyne and his colleagues (2001) found that in men and women with heart failure, high levels of marital conflict were associated with shorter survival time. This effect was present in both men and women, but conflict seemed to be a stronger predictor of dying for the female patients. In this research, marital quality was as good a predictor of how long people would live as an objective measure of how severe the heart failure was at the beginning of the study.

How does marital strife cause so much disease and death, especially by way of the heart? Perhaps the poets are correct: love lies in the heart, and love thwarted breaks the heart. But in physiological terms, we can consider other causes as well. Both men and women locked in hostile marriages have chronically elevated levels of fight-or-flight arousal, leading to bigger changes in heart rate and blood pressure whenever a conflict occurs (Robles and Kiecolt-Glaser 2003). People in unhappy relationships have stronger reactions to stress in the form of cortisol release than people in happy relationships. In fact, just thinking about their unhappy relationship caused large increases in cortisol levels in the saliva of people in one study (Berry and Worthington 2001).

A CLOSER LOOK AT SACRIFICE

A fascinating study by Emily Impett, Shelly Gable, and Letitia Peplau (2005) looked at the role of sacrifice in intimate relationships. All relationships involve some degree of sacrifice: he gives up a football game to take his wife on a picnic, she gives up seeing an eagerly anticipated movie to help him entertain clients. It's these little acts of (as the authors put it) "giving up and giving in" that make relationships work over the long haul—but only if the sacrifices are made for the right reasons. The evidence shows that if you yield in order to avoid nagging, a fight, or disapproval, you're actually setting yourself and your partner up for more anxiety and tension in the relationship. You may even be setting the stage for a breakup, according to Impett, Gable, and Peplau.

Sacrificing your interests because you want to make your partner happy tends to lead to more happiness and pleasure in the relationship. Impett, Gable, and Peplau speculate that this type of sacrifice is essentially an active coping technique, one in which you are going after what you want rather than trying to avoid what you don't want. As you learned in chapter 2, active coping is associated with better health and more positive moods than avoidant coping.

The lesson here is that it could be beneficial to ask yourself what motivates you to make sacrifices in your intimate relationships. Is it because you're afraid of being rejected? Is it because you want to avoid an argument? If you realize that your motives come from fear or avoidance, it might be time for a conversation with your partner about what you both want and need from each other. If there is a lot of conflict in the relationship, consider having this conversation with the help of a couples counselor, so there is a safe environment for the expression of any emotions that come up as a result of uncovering long-simmering resentments.

GOOD NEWS AND BAD NEWS ABOUT GOOD NEWS

Have you ever found that wonderful news just didn't seem real or true until you shared it with someone you loved, and sharing it only amplified your joy and excitement about your good fortune? This effect has been studied by Shelly Gable and her colleagues (2004). In several small research projects, Gable and her team examined the effects of sharing good news with an enthusiastic, supportive significant other. The data show that this act tends to increase your positive mood and your sense of well-being, and it also has benefits for the relationship, including making it more intimate.

How can you use this information? First, remember that the benefits were reaped only if the information was received with enthusiasm and support. So, if your loved one shares good news with you, be sure to communicate your genuine happiness. If you don't feel happy about your partner's good news, this may signal real problems in the relationship. Similarly, if your good news is frequently met by neutral, disinterested, or outright negative responses by your partner, there may be a real need to explore issues of intimacy, competitiveness, envy, and other possible problems in the relationship. In the long run, a lack of support for your good fortune can be almost as harmful to you and your relationship as a lack of support when things go wrong.

UNDERSTANDING COMMUNICATION STYLES

In his excellent book *Undoing Perpetual Stress* (2005), Richard O'Connor writes about the ways that communication styles can create problems in intimate relationships, especially those between men and women. In general, as O'Connor and others have pointed out, men take a pragmatic, problem-solving approach when discussing stressful events and life challenges. Women, on the other hand, tend to take comfort in processing the emotional ramifications of the stressor, seeking understanding interest when they discuss problems. These two communication styles are not strictly based in gender, however. Different people use different modes of communication and have different expectations and needs from their social networks when stressed. What matters is that you learn to recognize your own communication style and to ask for the type of support you need when you're under stress.

Exercise: Ask for What You Want

Here's an exercise to help you identify your social support preferences and needs. You'll need your notebook for this exercise. Begin by remembering a stressful incident that occurred in the last week or two. Choose something that you told someone about after it happened. It doesn't have to be a dramatic event, just something that bothered you. Now, write a paragraph about the incident.

After you're done, take a minute to reread what you just wrote, and answer the following questions:

1. Did you write a dry narrative based on the facts?

2. Did you write about how you felt as the event was happening?

3. Did you write about blame or responsibility for the event, ascribing it either to yourself or to someone or something outside of yourself?

4. Did you include a lot of sensory detail in your story?

Now, think about the person you told the story to. Describe your relationship with this person in a line or two. Now, thinking back, how did you tell the story to this person? Answer the same four questions about that conversation. Finally, note the response you got from the person you shared the story with, keeping these things in mind:

1. Did the person express sympathy?

2. Did the person offer you advice?

3. Did the person ask questions about how you were feeling?

4. Did the person ask for more factual information?

5. During your conversation, did the other person's emotional tone match yours?

6. Were you satisfied with the conversation? Did you feel heard and supported?

7. Did you feel that the person cared about you and your problem?

By analyzing what you've written, you can get some insight into your style of social support seeking and whether your needs are being met. Looking at the first set of questions, notice whether you described the event in emotional or factual terms. Focusing on blame or responsibility may trigger a greater need for practical processing of the event, to get the facts straight and do a reality check so you don't end up feeling unnecessarily responsible or preoccupied with having been wronged. If you had a lot of sensory detail in your story, the event may have been a traumatic experience that you need to process emotionally to better organize and store the memory to make it less disturbing.

Now, look at the way you told the story to your friend, partner, or family member. Was it in the same style as your written story? If not, you may be changing your delivery in an attempt to match what you perceive as your partner's style of coping with stress. This may be helpful in getting your point across, but it may not elicit the type of support you need. If you're feeling upset but you need to tell your story in dry, factual terms to get the other person to listen to you, you may be missing out on the emotional validation and comfort you're looking for.

Look at your analysis of the other person's response. This will give you more information about the degree of compatibility you have with your confidante. If you were looking for emotional succor and the person asked for factual information and gave advice, you may have been frustrated and disappointed by the encounter. Consider the idea that often, people are giving you what they think will be helpful, based on what helps them.

You can't change the way your family, friends, and partner manage and process stress. But you can help them give you the type of social support you need. Using the information from this exercise, reflect on what it is that helps you most when you're stressed. Think about who in your life can give it to you. Sometimes, advice is just what's needed to get through a tough situation. At other times, a hug and a warm conversation are best. You'll be most successful at reaping the benefits of social support if you develop the self-awareness to know what you need and where to get it. It helps to start with the assumption that your partner and friends want to give you what you need. Starting from that assumption makes it easier to ask, and it gives them the opportunity to make you happy and strengthen the relationship. If this assumption is proven wrong, then it may be time to look deeper at whether this relationship is healthy and what needs to be done to make it so.

Conclusion

Relationships help you define, create, and express yourself. They have the power to help you thrive, or to hurt you in ways that are sometimes overt and sometimes subtle. As you work on your communication skills and your self-awareness, you'll be able to make and cultivate connections with people that make you happier and healthier, and you'll be able to know when it's time to let toxic, harmful relationships go.

9

Be a Master of Cool, Even When It's Hot

Most of us can't make major changes in our lives to make them less stressful. We have jobs, kids, mortgages, bills, relatives, and other things we have to attend to, and all these can add to our stress levels. It makes sense to evaluate your lifestyle and see if you can't relieve some of the pressure by changing your priorities, working on your relationships, maybe even changing jobs. At some point, however, even after you've de-stressed your life as much as you can, you still need to cope with the everyday hassles, hassles you now know can add up to chronic stress and health problems.

As you learned in the introduction, the acute stress response is highly adaptive and lifesaving, but expensive in terms of the resources your body needs to heal, grow, regenerate, and nourish itself. Animals in their natural environments move in and out of these acute stress reactions naturally, but we humans, with our ability to ruminate and fret over our problems, often get locked into a stress response that goes on and on.

Mind-Body Techniques for Stress Management

Most mind-body medicine techniques have the same goal: to shift you from an activated, stressed state to a calm, relaxed state. This helps you in at least two ways. First, it gives you a break while you're doing it. Second, regular practice of one of several relaxation techniques leads to less nervous system activation the rest of the day, counteracting the harmful health effects of stress and hassles. Let's take a look at four mind-body techniques you can use every day.

THE RELAXATION RESPONSE

Herbert Benson introduced the relaxation response in 1975 as a way to induce a deeply relaxed state similar to that of meditation. Benson and his colleagues have done extensive research into the immediate physical effects and long-term health benefits of this technique. One important discovery is that during the relaxation response, there are big reductions in oxygen consumption by the body, reflecting a state of deep rest and relaxation (Friedman et al. 1996).

The technique is easy to learn. To elicit the relaxation response, you need only take two steps: First, focus your awareness on a phrase, a sound, or a word. Second, stay with your focus even when thoughts arise. Gently dismiss any intruding thoughts and return to your word or phrase. That's it. It's best to practice for ten to twenty minutes a day—and it does take practice. You may find it difficult to let those intruding thoughts go without getting attached to them, but as you learn to do that, you'll also be learning to relax your body and mind in a profound way that can have wide-ranging benefits.

BREATH WORK

Breathing is a unique bodily function that happens at the boundary between your *autonomic* (previously thought of as automatic, beyond your control) and voluntary nervous systems. You can decide how to breathe, but you don't stop breathing when you stop thinking about it. Shallow, irregular, and rapid breathing is associated with stress, and can reinforce it. It's easy to learn how to make your breathing deeper, slower, and more regular, and this kind of breathing leads to pronounced relaxation that you can feel in your muscles and appreciate in your mind. It also lowers your blood pressure, slows your heart rate, and has good effects on your immune, nervous, and endocrine systems (DeGuire et al. 1996).

GUIDED IMAGERY

Doing guided imagery is like watching a movie in your mind. Your body will respond to the content of the movie, or the imagery. When you think of something that bothers you, your body reacts with a stress response. When you think of someone you love, you may involuntarily smile and feel your hands get warmer. This is your body relaxing and entering a state of well-being, guided by your imagination. The power of imagery can be harmful (when you have disturbing memories and stressful thoughts) and helpful (when you purposely imagine pleasant, healing things to help your body relax). Guided imagery can be passive, when a script is read by a therapist or from a recording, or active, when you choose a situation and imagine it happening.

Imagery work can produce powerful physiological changes, including strong influences on immune function (Achterberg and Rider 1989). It can also help you gain insight into stressful situations and physical problems. Imagery work enhances emotional awareness, relieves anxiety, and reduces pain related to various illnesses and medical procedures (Syrjala, Cummings, and Donaldson 1992; Walker et al. 1999).

AUTOGENIC TRAINING

Your nervous system is being triggered repeatedly by stressful thoughts and hassles. You can solve this problem in two ways. One is to address the thoughts and put the hassles in perspective so they don't bother you any more. You can work on that using many of the techniques you've learned in this book. The other piece is to start training your nervous system to be less reactive to stressful input.

Autogenic training is a form of self-hypnosis in which you train your nervous system to calm down whenever you want it to. It's a reliable, powerful tool for relaxation that most of my clients and students really enjoy. The idea is that you practice the technique in a safe, relaxed environment for a few weeks. Then you start using it in your daily life.

If you've ever had a puppy, you know something about training. You want him to learn to sit, so what do you do? You start at home, patiently saying sit and guiding his body into a sitting position. Then you give him a reward. Gradually, he gets to the point where he will sit with only the verbal cue; you don't have to guide him any more. Eventually, you don't have to give him a treat every time—a simple "Good boy!" is enough of a reward to keep him sitting for you. Then you can take the show on the road. Take him to the park and let him run around and make friends with the other dogs, having a ball. You may have to go back to using treats and physical guidance to remind him to sit when you tell him to, but in time, you can even get him to listen to you when he's distracted or busy with other things.

That is how autogenic training works for you. You practice it at home, learning simple commands and associating them with imagery to make the commands more integrated with your brain's way of communicating. You find that you're able to get relaxed easily using the commands after a few weeks, and then you can take it on the road. Get to the office, see a pile of papers that need your attention, notice your muscles starting to tense up, and what do you do? Tell your inner puppy to sit. And it will.

Exercise: Autogenic Training

Practice this technique every day, at the same time of day. It really doesn't matter when you practice, as long as you know you won't be interrupted and the environment is comfortable. You can do this on your lunch break at work or at home when you get up. Sit in a comfortable chair. I don't recommend lying down, because it's best not to fall asleep while you're learning the technique. Later, however, you can use it to help yourself get to sleep if you have insomnia.

Begin by closing your eyes and focusing on your body and how it feels. Briefly run from head to toes, noting whether you need to loosen your clothes or adjust your position so your muscles can relax. Once you're comfortable, shift your attention to your breathing. Pay attention to the air coming into your lungs, filling your chest, and slowly moving out of your body, carrying away things you don't need. Think about your breath getting a little slower and deeper, but don't force it to change. It's remarkable how your breath will settle on its own just because you're paying attention to it. If thoughts come into your head (and they will), tell yourself you'll deal with them later.

Just say *Not now*, and let the thoughts wander off. Don't try to suppress them, because that will only make them more persistent.

Now, repeat these phrases to yourself three each. While you're repeating the phrases, create an image in your mind of the thing happening. For example, for *My hands are soft and warm*, you might imagine them cupped around a bowl of soup. Use more than one sense. What does it look like? How does it smell? Make the imagery for each suggestion as detailed and vivid as possible, and your body will respond more fully to it. At first, it may be hard to remember the phrases, so you will have to look at this book, but it won't be long before you have them memorized. Remember, say each one three times to yourself before moving on to the next one.

My hands are soft and warm ... I am at peace.
My legs are heavy and warm ... I am at peace.
My breathing is deep and calm ... I am at peace.
My forehead is cool ... I am at peace.
My belly is soft and warm ... I am at peace.
My body is always healing itself ... I am at peace.

Before you open your eyes and come back to your regular state of awareness, take a minute to scan your body again and notice how it feels to be deeply relaxed. The more familiar you get with this feeling, the easier it will be for you to recognize when you need to create it.

After you've practiced daily for a couple of weeks, try using autogenic training out in the world in situations that normally cause you stress. The easiest way to do this is to choose the phrase you like best and make it a sort of mantra. I personally like *I am at peace*, or *I am peace*. When I'm in traffic or another stressful situation, I interrupt my busy mind and focus on my hands. I think about them getting warm, and I say *I am at peace* to myself. In moments, my hands get warmer and I feel calmer. My puppy sits down once again.

Conclusion

There are many skills available to you for stress management. Which one you choose is not as important as whether you choose one and master it. It's unfortunate that we don't learn these skills as children, as a matter of course—but it's never too late. Knowing how to calm yourself when you need it is a powerful way to take charge of your body, your mind, and your health. You can learn more about mind-body medicine at www.cmbm.org.

Rise Above It

Stressful events are all around you all the time. All you need to do is look: watch the news on television, walk down a city street, ponder the rising cost of gasoline. There are opportunities for anxiety and despair everywhere, yet many people seem to be able to put it all in perspective and continue growing, thriving, and being happy, even in the worst of circumstances. How do they do it? Thriving is served, for many people, by a sense of wonder, inspiration, awe, and connection with a greater aspect of reality than what is immediately obvious. These things add up to spirituality and often are acted out as religion. You can integrate these benefits into your life regardless of your particular beliefs.

The Basic Human Strength of Transcendence

Transcendence may be the key to developing a spiritual orientation to life. Transcendent experience has been defined many ways, but it often includes the extension of the boundaries of the self beyond the physical body, either to vast spaces within or through connection with infinite space beyond the individual. The experience is rarely frightening, and usually brings with it a sense of profound connection and well-being. People who have had transcendent experiences report that they felt like they were part of a larger existence, and this gave them a sense of purpose and control over everyday life (Waldfogel 1997).

Transcendence has also been identified as a basic human strength in the new field of positive psychology, which focuses on what's good and strong about human psychology rather than what's wrong with us. According to positive psychology researchers Chris Peterson and Martin Seligman (2004), the elements of transcendence are appreciation of beauty, gratitude, hope, humor, and spirituality. Humor may seem like an odd thing to add to this mix of human qualities, but when you think about it, having a sense of humor is a wonderful way to transcend life's hardships. "Someday we'll look back on this and laugh." That's a very spiritual thing to say; it has hope, gratitude, faith, and a sense of comforting togetherness to it. There's the assumption that we can survive hardship and grow from it—and, from the perspective of that newfound wisdom, see the humor in what today seems like a bad thing.

The Health Benefits of Spirituality and Religion

There has been an explosion of interest in the ways that spirituality and religion can improve health and long-term well-being. Research suggests that religious and spiritual experience can have both physiological and psychological benefits. How can this be? How can a sense of wonder and connection to divinity or attendance at church services create measurable changes in physiology? And what does this understanding tell us about how we should live?

HOW DO YOU MEASURE RELIGION AND SPIRITUALITY?

One problem with doing research on religion and spirituality is figuring out how to define these terms and measure the degree to which a person is spiritual or religious. We all know people who go to church every Sunday but behave in unkind ways the rest of the week. Are those people religious? Are they spiritual?

Let's look at a few variables to consider. Some studies look at behavior. This would include attending services, using religious coping behaviors, praying or meditating regularly, or seeking social support in a religious context. We could also look at a person's thoughts and feelings with respect to religion and spirit. These are things like perceived closeness to God, finding benefit in spiritual acts, having a sense of meaning in life, and the strength of the person's faith in a deity or set of teachings.

It's important to keep in mind that each study of religion and spirituality may have defined these terms differently. Interestingly, Teresa Seeman, Linda Dubin, and Melvin Seeman (2003) point out that most of the research has not focused on participation in Judeo-Christian religion and spirituality, which is significant because so many people in the United States participate in it. Most of the research has instead focused on meditation.

BIOLOGY, RELIGION, AND SPIRITUALITY

People who engage in religious and spiritual activities experience benefits to many body systems, including the cardiovascular, nervous, endocrine, and immune systems. Several studies of religion and spirituality have shown a beneficial effect of religious practice on blood pressure. As people get more involved in religious activities like attending church, feeling committed to religion, or becoming a nun, they experience a lower incidence of high blood pressure (Seeman, Dubin, and Seeman 2003). People who have a long-term practice of meditation also tend to have lower rates of hypertension (Schneider et al. 1995). Church attendance in general seems to be associated with living longer and having lower rates of many chronic illnesses (Waldfogel 1997). Scoring high on measures of religiousness or spirituality is associated with better immune function and less cardiovascular reactivity to stressful events (Seeman, Dubin, and Seeman 2003).

Nobody is sure exactly how religious activity, spirituality, and physiological function are connected. Perhaps going to church is a relaxing experience similar to a session of meditation, with long-lasting physical effects. Perhaps being spiritually oriented contributes to better mood states; we know that positive mood states tend to protect against stress-related physical changes.

PSYCHOLOGY, RELIGION, AND SPIRITUALITY

Religion and spirituality have psychological benefits as well as physiological ones. In their study of older adults, Paul Wink and Michele Dillon (2003) looked at the benefits of both religiousness and spirituality. They defined religiousness as a belief in God and the afterlife, adherence to institutionalized religious beliefs, and attendance at traditional places of worship. They found that being a religious person seems to inspire more social and community involvement, and this enhanced involvement in the world leads to higher levels of social support and feelings of accomplishment. Wink and Dillon measured spirituality by asking people about their nontraditional beliefs and practices that were relevant to connection with a sacred other. People who rated high on spirituality appeared to be different in some ways from the religious people. Highly spiritual people exhibited high levels of well-being that came from personal growth. They also tended to be very involved in pursuing knowledge and creative endeavors. Both groups were experiencing benefits from their beliefs and practices, only in different ways.

What's the active ingredient in religiousness and spirituality that is responsible for these positive effects? Most likely, it is a heightened sense of meaning and coherence in the world. Meaning-based coping is recognized as a highly adaptive strategy that can lead to better moods and healthier behaviors. A sense of spiritual meaning appears to be protective against depression (Mascaro and Rosen 2006). It may be that viewing life as a coherent, meaningful enterprise gives people a stronger sense of purpose, because their intentions and beliefs guide behaviors and provide a rationale for the choices they make.

There are many definitions of spirituality, but they all seem to include some sense of a reality that transcends everyday experience. When life's stresses and problems are put in a bigger perspective—eternity, ultimate truth, ultimate goodness, heaven and hell—they seem smaller and, for many people, somehow more manageable. Identifying with that bigness can help you feel more able to endure and learn from the petty grievances you have to suffer every day.

What does this mean for you? Perhaps, if your score was low, you might want to cultivate a sense of spiritual connection and meaning in your life. There are many ways to do that, from reading books about spirituality to finding a community to join, to taking a yoga class, to joining a church. It's up to you, but if you feel drawn to it, you will be able to find some way to nurture your spiritual longing.

Exercise: Does Life Have Meaning?

In their study of college undergraduates, Nathan Mascaro and David Rosen (2006) sought links between spirituality, stress, and depression. The questionnaire they used is reproduced here, with the authors' permission, so you can assess your sense of spiritual meaning.

For each item, circle the number that corresponds with the degree to which you agree with the statement.

There is no particular reason why I exist.

I totally disagree			I totally agree	
5	4	3	2	1

We are meant to make our own special contribution to the world.

I totally disagree			I totally agree	
1	2	3	4	5

I was meant to actualize my potentials.

I totally disagree			I totally agree	
1	2	3	4	5

Life is inherently meaningful.

I totally disagree			I totally agree	
1	2	3	4	5

I will never have a spiritual bond with anyone.

I totally disagree			I totally agree	
5	4	3	2	1

When I look deep within my heart, I see a life I am compelled to pursue.

I totally disagree			I totally agree	
1	2	3	4	5

My life is meaningful.

I totally disagree			I totally agree	
1	2	3	4	5

In performing certain tasks, I can feel something higher or transcendent working through me.

I totally disagree			I totally agree	
1	2	3	4	5

Our flawed and often horrific behavior indicates that there is little or no meaning inherent in our existence.

I totally disagree			I totally agree	
5	4	3	2	1

I find meaning even in my mistakes and sins.

I totally disagree			I totally agree	
1	2	3	4	5

I see a special purpose for myself in this world.

I totally disagree			I totally agree	
1	2	3	4	5

There are certain activities, jobs, or services to which I feel called.

I totally disagree			I totally agree	
1	2	3	4	5

There is no reason or meaning underlying human existence.

I totally disagree			I totally agree	
5	4	3	2	1

Something purposeful is at the heart of this world.

| I totally disagree | | | I totally agree | |
| 1 | 2 | 3 | 4 | 5 |

We are all participating in something larger and greater than any of us.

| I totally disagree | | | I totally agree | |
| 1 | 2 | 3 | 4 | 5 |

Now, add up the number values of your responses to get your score. The average score in the study by Mascaro and Rosen was 63. When people scored above 63, they showed more resiliency in the face of stress in that they had fewer symptoms of depression in response to daily stressors. People who scored at 52 or less tended to develop depressive symptoms more easily as the stress in their lives increased.

Enhancing Spirituality

The fundamental ability to cultivate spirituality in daily life has even been measured in medical research. In a study by James Kennedy, Anne Abbott, and Beth Rosenberg (2002), cardiac patients and their spouses were taken on a two-and-a-half-day educational retreat to learn about improving lifestyle in the presence of cardiac disease. The program included yoga, meditation, imagery, and prayer. After the retreat was over, 78 percent of the people who attended reported an increase in their level of spirituality. To the extent that people became more spiritual, they also reported higher levels of well-being, a greater sense of meaning in life, and more confidence in their ability to handle problems in life. It's quite possible that the people on the retreat were primed for a sort of spiritual awakening simply because they were dealing with a life-threatening disease. Nevertheless, the study suggests that spiritual growth and awareness is available to you always, and you can explore it anytime, without waiting for that wake-up call in the form of stress or illness.

Prayer is a form of spiritual practice that doesn't have to be aligned with any particular religion, although it is a mainstay of pretty much every religion on earth. There are different types of prayer, including *petitionary* prayer (asking for something) and *meditative* or *contemplative* prayer (being in the presence of the divine). There are many documented benefits of prayer of both types. More important than the type of prayer is how it feels when you're doing it (Poloma and Pendleton 1991). If it leads to a greater sense of connection and meaning, it's probably having a beneficial effect.

Prayer is something you can do anytime, anywhere. All you need to do is sit quietly and allow your mind to slow down. Decide ahead of time what kind of prayer you want to do. Many of the people I've worked with start with prayers of thanksgiving. I think this is a beautiful way to start a prayer practice. It can be as simple as bowing your head briefly before you eat. Expressing gratitude is a great way to remind yourself that your life is a miracle, and no matter what's going on, things could be worse.

I have a simple ritual that I do every morning. I light a candle and read something inspirational, usually some Buddhist dharma. I contemplate what I have just read for a couple of minutes while gazing at the flame. This helps maintain my focus on the moment. After I feel I've absorbed some of the wisdom of the dharma reading, I close my eyes and ask for help in living this day in a way that is worthy of the gift of being alive. I take a few slow, deep breaths, and that's it. I'm on my way to my daily life, but somehow the entire day is elevated to a new level of meaning from those few moments of connection.

Conclusion

Joan Borysenko is a wise, funny, generous person who has made landmark contributions to the art and science of mind-body medicine. Throughout her career she's been a scholar, a teacher, a healer, and a writer. She's also a wonderful public speaker. In recent years, she's turned her creativity and energy to encouraging people to incorporate more spirituality into their lives. Her book *Inner Peace for Busy People* (2001) is a wonderful resource for building a spiritual life, written for people who think they don't have the time for it. In the introduction to the book, Borysenko writes, "Every day brings a choice: to practice stress or to practice peace" (xvii). This is a nugget of wisdom to hold on to. Being spiritual, adopting a religious practice, being a stressed-out maniac—these are all choices we make from moment to moment. It's up to you to exert whatever control you can to make your life as peaceful, as generous, and as happy as it can be.

References

Abramson, J. L., and V. Vaccarino. 2002. Relationship between physical activity and inflammation among apparently healthy middle-aged and older U.S. adults. *Archives of Internal Medicine* 162(11):1286–92.

Achterberg, J., and M. S. Rider. 1989. The effect of music-mediated imagery on neutrophils and lymphocytes. *Biofeedback and Self-Regulation* 14:247–57.

Aldwin, C. M., and C. L. Park. 2004. Coping and physical health outcomes: An overview. *Psychology and Health* 19(3):277–81.

Altman, D. 1990. *Art of the Inner Meal.* New York: HarperCollins.

Arnsten, A. 1998. The biology of being frazzled. *Science* 12:1711-1712.

Aspinwall, L. G., and S. E. Taylor. 1997. A stitch in time: Self-regulation and proactive coping. *Psychological Bulletin* 121(3):417–36.

Astin, J. A. 1997. Stress reduction through mindfulness meditation: Effects on psychological symptomatology, sense of control, and spiritual experiences. *Psychotherapy and Psychosomatics* 66(2):97–106.

Benson, H. 1975. *The Relaxation Response.* New York: William Morrow.

Berry, J. W., and E. L. Worthington. 2001. Forgivingness, relationship quality, stress while imagining relationship events, and physical and mental health. *Journal of Counseling Psychology* 48(4): 447–55.

Blair, S. N., Y. Cheng, and J. S. Holder. 2001. Is physical activity or physical fitness more important in defining health benefits. *Medicine and Science in Sports and Exercise* 33:S379–99.

Blair, S. N., H. W. Kohl, R. S. Paffenbarger, D. G. Clark, K. H. Cooper, and L. W. Gibbons. 1989. Physical fitness and all-cause mortality: A prospective study of healthy men and women. *Journal of the American Medical Association* 262(17):2395–2401.

Boggiano, M. M., P. C. Chandler, J. B. Viana, K. D. Oswald, C. R. Maldonado, and P. K. Wauford. 2005. Combined dieting and stress evoke exaggerated responses to opioids in binge-eating rats. *Behavioral Neuroscience* 119(5):1207–14.

Borysenko, J. Z. 2001. *Inner Peace for Busy People: 52 Simple Strategies for Transforming Your Life.* Carlsbad, CA: Hay House.

Burns, V. E., D. Carroll, C. Ring, L. K. Harrison, and M. Drayson. 2002. Stress, coping, and hepatitis B antibody status. *Psychosomatic Medicine* 64:287–93.

Buss, D. M. 2000. The evolution of happiness. *American Psychologist* 55(1):15–23.

Butler, E. A., B. Egloff, F. H. Wilhelm, N. C. Smith, E. A. Erickson, and J. J. Gross. 2003. The social consequences of expressive suppression. *Emotion* 3:48–67.

Cahn, B. R., and J. Polich. 2006. Meditation states and traits: EEG, ERP, and neuroimaging studies. *Psychological Bulletin* 132(2):180–211.

Caprara, G. V., and P. Steca. 2005. Affective and social self-regulatory efficacy beliefs as determinants of positive thinking and happiness. *European Psychologist* 10(4):275–86.

Carver, C. S. 1997. You want to measure coping but your protocol's too long: Consider the Brief COPE. *International Journal of Behavioral Medicine* 4:92–100.

Carver, C. S., and M. F. Scheier. 2002. Optimism. In *Handbook of Positive Psychology*, edited by C. R. Snyder and S. J. Lopez. New York: Oxford University Press.

Centers for Disease Control. 2003. Prevalence of physical activity, including lifestyle activities among adults—United States, 2000–2001. *Morbidity and Mortality Weekly* 52(32): 764–69.

Compton, W. C. 2001. Toward a tripartite factor structure of mental health: Subjective well-being, personal growth, and religiosity. *Journal of Psychology* 135(5):486–500.

Coyne, J. C., M. J. Rohrbaugh, V. Shoham, J. S. Sonnega, J. M. Nicklas, and J. A. Cranford. 2001. Prognostic importance of marital quality for survival of congestive heart failure. *American Journal of Cardiology* 88:526–29.

Csikszentmihalyi, M. 1997. *Finding Flow: The Psychology of Engagement with Everyday Life*. New York: Basic Books.

Dallman, M. F., S. E. la Fleur, N. Pecoraro, F. Gomez, H. Houshyar, and S. F. Akana. 2004. Minireview: Glucocorticoids—food intake, abdominal obesity, and wealthy nations in 2004. *Endocrinology* 145(6):2633–38.

de Becker, G. 1997. *The Gift of Fear and Other Survival Signals That Protect Us from Violence*. New York: Dell Publishing.

DeGuire, S., R. Gevirtz, D. Hawkinson, and K. Dixon. 1996. Breathing retraining: A three-year follow-up study of treatment for hyperventilation syndrome and associated functional cardiac symptoms. *Biofeedback and Self-Regulation* 21(2):191–98.

DeLongis, A., S. Folkman, and R. S. Lazarus. 1988. The impact of daily stress on health and mood: Psychological and social resources as mediators. *Journal of Personality and Social Psychology* 54(3):486–95.

Dimeo, F., M. Bauer, I. Varahram, G. Proest, and U. Halter. 2001. Benefits from aerobic exercise in patients with major depression: A pilot study. *British Journal of Sports Medicine* 35:114–17.

Droste, S. K., A. Gesing, S. Ulbricht, M. B. Muller, A. C. E. Linthorst, and J. M. H. M. Reul. 2003. Effects of long-term voluntary exercise on the mouse hypothalamic-pituitary-adrenocortical axis. *Endocrinology* 144(7):3012–23.

Dua, J. K. 1994. Comparative predictive value of attributional style, negative affect, and positive affect in predicting self-reported physical health and psychological health. *Journal of Psychosomatic Research* 38(7):669–80.

Epel, E. S., E. H. Blackburn, J. Lin, F. S. Dhabhar, N. E. Adler, J. D. Morrow, and R. M. Cawthon. 2004. From the Cover: Accelerated telomere shortening in response to life stress. *Proceedings of the National Academy of Science* 101(49):17312–15.

Epel, E., R. Lapidus, B. McEwen, and K. D. Brownell. 2001. Stress may add bite to appetite in women: A laboratory study of stress-induced cortisol and eating behavior. *Psychoneuroendocrinology* 26:37–49.

Epel, E., B. McEwen, T. Seeman, K. Matthews, G. Castellazzo, K. D. Brownell, J. Bell, and J. R. Ickovics. 2000. Stress and body shape: Stress-induced cortisol secretion is consistently greater among women with central fat. *Psychosomatic Medicine* 62(5):623–32.

Fernstrom, M. H., and J. D. Fernstrom. 1995. Brain tryptophan concentrations and serotonin synthesis remain responsive to food consumption after the ingestion of sequential meals. *American Journal of Clinical Nutrition* 61(2):312–19.

Folkman, S., R. S. Lazarus, R. J. Gruen, and A. DeLongis. 1986. Appraisal, coping, health status, and psychological status. *Journal of Personality and Social Psychology* 50(3):571–79.

Fontana, A., and S. Badawy. 1997. Perceptual and coping processes across the menstrual cycle: An investigation in PMS clinic and community samples. *Behavioral Medicine* 22(4):152–59.

Fontana, A., and M. McLaughlin. 1998. Coping and appraisal of daily stressors predict heart rate and blood pressure levels in young women. *Behavioral Medicine* 24:5–16.

Friedman, R., P. Myers, S. Krass, and H. Benson. 1996. The relaxation response: Use with cardiac patients. In *Heart and Mind: The Practice of Cardiac Psychology*, edited by R. Allan and S. Scheidt. Washington, DC: American Psychological Association.

Fuller, J. A., J. M. Stanton, G. G. Fisher, C. Spitzmuller, S. S. Russell, and P. C. Smith. 2003. A lengthy look at the daily grind: Time series analysis of events, mood, stress, and satisfaction. *Journal of Applied Psychology* 88(6):1019–33.

Gable, S. L., H. T. Reis, E. A. Impett, and E. R. Asher. 2004. What do you do when things go right? The intrapersonal and interpersonal benefits of sharing positive events. *Journal of Personality and Social Psychology* 87(2):228–45.

Georgiades, A., A. Sherwood, E. C. D. Gullette, M. A. Babyak, A. Hinderliter, R. Waugh, D. Tweedy, L. Craighead, R. Bloomer, and J. A. Blumenthal. 2000. Effects of exercise and weight loss on mental stress–induced cardiovascular responses in individuals with high blood pressure. *Hypertension* 36:171–76.

Giese-Davis, J., S. E. Sephton, H. C. Abercrombie, R. E. F. Duran, and D. Spiegel. 2004. Repression and high anxiety are associated with aberrant diurnal cortisol rhythms in women with metastatic breast cancer. *Health Psychology* 23:645–50.

Glaser, R. 2005. Stress-associated immune dysregulation and its importance for human health: A personal history of psychoneuroimmunology. *Brain, Behavior, and Immunity* 19:3–11.

Goldbacher, E. M., K. Matthews, and K. Salomon. 2005. Central adiposity is associated with cardiovascular reactivity to stress in adolescents. *Health Psychology* 24(4):375–84.

Grassi, L., R. Righi, L. Sighinolfi, S. Makoui, and F. Ghinelli. 1998. Coping styles and psychosocial-related variables in HIV-infected patients. *Psychosomatics* 39:350–59.

Harp, D., and N. Feldman. 1996. *The Three-Minute Meditator: 30 Simple Ways to Unwind Your Mind and Enhance Your Emotional Intelligence.* New York: MJF Books.

Harrison, K., and A. L. Marske. 2005. Nutritional content of foods advertised during the television programs children watch most. *American Journal of Public Health* 95(9): 1568–74.

Hawkley, L. C., G. G. Berntson, C. G. Engeland, P. T. Marucha, C. M. Masi, and J. T. Cacioppo. 2005. Stress, aging, and resilience: Can accrued wear and tear be slowed? *Canadian Psychology* 46(3):115–25.

Heaney, C. A., and B. A. Israel. 1997. Social networks and social support. In *Health Behavior and Health Education: Theory, Research, and Practice,* edited by K. Glanz, B. Rimer, and F. Lewis. San Francisco: Jossey-Bass.

Hedley, A. A., C. L. Ogden, C. L. Johnson, M. D. Carroll, L. R. Curtin, and K. M. Flegal. 2004. Prevalence of overweight and obesity among U.S. children, adolescents, and adults, 1999– 2002. *Journal of the American Medical Association* 291(23):2847–50.

Holahan, C. J., R. H. Moos, C. K. Holahan, P. L. Brennan, and K. K. Schutte. 2005. Stress generation, avoidance coping, and depressive symptoms: A 10-year model. *Journal of Consulting and Clinical Psychology* 73(4):658–66.

Holmes, T. H., and R. H. Rahe. 1967. The Social Readjustment Rating Scale. *Journal of Psychosomatic Research* 11:213–18.

Impett, E. A., S. L. Gable, and L. A. Peplau. 2005. Giving up and giving in: The costs and benefits of daily sacrifice in intimate relationships. *Journal of Personality and Social Psychology* 89(3):327–44.

Isen, A. M. 2003. Positive affect as a source of human strength. In *A Psychology of Human Strengths: Fundamental Questions and Future Directions for a Positive Psychology,* edited by L. Aspinwall and U. Staudinger. Washington, DC: American Psychological Association.

Jakicic, J. M., C. Winters, W. Lang, and R. R. Wing. 1999. Effects of intermittent exercise and use of home exercise equipment on adherence, weight loss, and fitness in overweight women. *Journal of the American Medical Association* 282(16):1554–60.

Janoff-Bulman, R. 1992. *Shattered Assumptions: Towards a New Psychology of Trauma.* New York: Free Press.

Kabat-Zinn, J. 1990. *Full Catastrophe Living.* New York: Delta.

Kabat-Zinn, J., L. Lipworth, R. Burney, and W. Sellers. 1987. Four-year follow-up of a meditation-based program for the self-regulation of chronic pain: Treatment outcomes and compliance. *Clinical Journal of Pain* 2:159–73.

Kabat-Zinn, J., A. O. Massion, J. Kristeller, L. G. Peterson, K. E. Fletcher, L. Pbert, W. R. Lenderking, and S. F. Santorelli. 1992. Effectiveness of a meditation-based stress reduction program in the treatment of anxiety disorders. *American Journal of Psychiatry* 149(7):936–43.

Kabat-Zinn, J., E. Wheeler, T. Light, A. Skillings, M. J. Scharf, T. G. Cropley, D. Hosmer, and J. D. Bernhard. 1998. Influence of a mindfulness meditation–based stress reduction intervention on rates of skin clearing in patients with moderate to severe psoriasis undergoing phototherapy (UVB) and photochemotherapy (PUVA). *Psychosomatic Medicine* 60(5):625–32.

Kahana, E., R. H. Lawrence, B. Kahana, K. Kercher, A. Wisniewski, E. Stoller, J. Tobin, and K. Stange. 2002. Long-term impact of preventive proactivity on quality of life of the old-old. *Psychosomatic Medicine* 64(3):382–94.

Kanaley, J. A., J. Y. Weltman, K. S. Pieper, A. Weltman, and M. L. Hartman. 2001. Cortisol and growth hormone responses to exercise at different times of day. *Journal of Clinical Endocrinology and Metabolism* 86:2881–89.

Kant, A. 2000. Consumption of energy-dense, nutrient-poor foods by adult Americans: Nutritional and health implications. The third National Health and Nutrition Examination

Survey, 1988–1994. *American Journal of Clinical Nutrition* 72:929–36.

Kaplan, K. H., D. L. Goldenberg, and M. Galvin-Nadeau. 1993. The impact of a meditation-based stress reduction program on fibromyalgia. *General Hospital Psychiatry* 15:284–89.

Kennedy, J. E., R. A. Abbott, and B. S. Rosenberg. 2002. Changes in spirituality and well-being in a retreat program for cardiac patients. *Alternative Therapies* 8(4):64–73.

Kiecolt-Glaser, J. K., G. G. Page, P. T. Marucha, R. C. MacCallum, and R. Glaser. 1998. Psychological influences on surgical recovery: Perspectives from psychoneuro-immunology. *American Psychologist* 53:1209–18.

Klein, K. 2002. Stress, expressive writing, and working memory. In *The Writing Cure: How Expressive Writing Promotes Health and Emotional Well-Being*, edited by S. Lepore and J. Smyth. Washington, DC: American Psychological Association.

Kohler, C. L., and L. Fish. 2002. The relationship of perceived self-efficacy to quality of life in chronic obstructive pulmonary disease. *Health Psychology* 21(6):610-614.

Kouvonen, A., M. Kivimaki, S. J. Cox, T. Cox, and J. Vahtera. 2005. Relationship between work stress and body mass index among 45,810 female and male employees. *Psychosomatic Medicine* 67(4):577–83.

Krohne, H. W., and K. E. Slangen. 2005. Influence of social support on adaptation to surgery. *Health Psychology* 24(1):101–5.

Kutz, I., J. Z. Borysenko, and H. Benson. 1985. Meditation and psychotherapy: A rationale for the integration of dynamic psychotherapy, the relaxation response, and mindfulness meditation. *American Journal of Psychiatry* 142(1):1–8.

Lampe, J. W. 1999. Health effects of vegetables and fruit: Assessing mechanisms of action in human experimental studies. *American Journal of Clinical Nutrition* 70(suppl.): 475S–490S.

Larson, M. R., R. Ader, and J. A. Moynihan. 2001. Heart rate, neuroendocrine, and immunological reactivity in response to an acute laboratory stressor. *Psychosomatic Medicine* 63(3):493–501.

Ledikwe, J. H., J. A. Ello-Martin, and B. J. Rolls. 2005. Portion sizes and the obesity epidemic. *Journal of Nutrition* 135:905–9.

Le Fur, C., M. Romon, P. Lebel, P. Devos, A. Lancry, L. Guedon-Moreau, J. Fruchart, and J. Dallongeville. 1999. Influence of mental stress and circadian cycle on post-prandial lipemia. *American Journal of Clinical Nutrition* 70:213-220.

Levine, A. S., C. M. Kotz, and B. A. Gosnell. 2003. Sugars: Hedonic aspects, neuroregulation, and energy balance. *American Journal of Clinical Nutrition* 78(4 suppl.): 834S–842S.

Lopez-Garcia, E., M. B. Schulze, J. B. Meigs, J. E. Manson, N. Rifai, M. J. Stampfer, W. C. Willett, and F. B. Hu. 2005. Consumption of trans fatty acids is related to plasma biomarkers of inflammation and endothelial dysfunction. *Journal of Nutrition* 135:562–66.

Manson, J. E., F. B. Hu, J. W. Rich-Edwards, G. A. Colditz, M. J. Stampfer, W. C. Willett, F. E. Speizer, and C. H. Hennekens. 1999. A prospective study of walking as compared with vigorous exercise in the prevention of coronary heart disease in women. *New England Journal of Medicine* 341:650–58.

Mascaro, N., and D. H. Rosen. 2006. The role of existential meaning as a buffer against stress. *Journal of Humanistic Psychology* 46(2):168–90.

Mayer, E. A. 2000. The neurobiology of stress and gastrointestinal disease. *Gut* 47:861–69.

Maynard, C. 2000. Association between week of the month and death from acute myocardial infarction in Washington state, 1988 to 1997. *American Heart Journal* 140(2):196–99.

McLean, J. A., S. I. Barr, and J. C. Prior. 2001. Cognitive dietary restraint is associated with higher urinary cortisol excretion in healthy premenopausal women. *American Journal of Clinical Nutrition* 73:7–12.

Miller, G. E., and S. Cohen. 2001. Psychological interventions and the immune system: A meta-analytic review and critique. *Health Psychology* 20:47–63.

Mor, N., and J. Winquist. 2002. Self-focused attention and negative affect: A meta-analysis. *Psychological Bulletin* 128(4): 638–62.

Nabkasorn, C., N. Miyai, A. Sootmongkol, S. Junprasert, H. Yamamoto, M. Arita, and K. Miyashita. 2006. Effects of physical exercise on depression, neuroendocrine stress hormones, and physiological fitness in adolescent females with depressive symptoms. *European Journal of Public Health* 16(2):179–84.

Ng, D. M., and R. W. Jeffery. 2003. Relationships between perceived stress and health behaviors in a sample of working adults. *Health Psychology* 22:638–42.

Nhãt Hanh, T. 1975. *The Miracle of Mindfulness: An Introduction to the Practice of Meditation*. Translated by M. Ho. Boston: Beacon Press.

O'Connor, R. 2005. *Undoing Perpetual Stress: The Missing Connection Between Depression, Anxiety, and Twenty-First Century Illness*. New York: Berkley Books.

Oettlé, G. J., P. M. Emmett, and K. W. Heaton. 1987. Glucose and insulin responses to manufactured and whole-food snacks. *American Journal of Clinical Nutrition* 45:86–91.

Oh, K., F. B. Hu, J. E. Manson, M. J. Stampfer, and W. C. Willett. 2005. Dietary fat intake and risk of coronary heart disease in women: 20 years of follow-up of the Nurses' Health Study. *American Journal of Epidemiology* 161(7): 672–79.

Oliver, G., J. Wardle, and E. L. Gibson. 2000. Stress and food choice: A laboratory study. *Psychosomatic Medicine* 62(6): 853–65.

Orth-Gomér, K., S. P. Wamala, M. Horsten, K. Schenck-Gustafsson, N. Schneiderman, and M. A. Mittleman. 2000. Marital stress worsens prognosis in women with coronary heart disease. *Journal of the American Medical Association* 284:3008–14.

Pederson, B. K., and L. Hoffman-Goetz. 2000. Exercise and the immune system: Regulation, integration, and adaptation. *Psychological Reviews* 80(3):1055–81.

Peirce, R. S., M. R. Frone, M. Russell, M. L. Cooper, and P. Mudar. 2000. A longitudinal model of social contact, social support, depression, and alcohol use. *Health Psychology* 19(1):28–38.

Perri, M. G., S. D. Anton, P. E. Durning, T. U. Ketterson, S. J. Sydeman, N. E. Berlant, W. F. Kanasky, R. L. Newton, M. C. Limacher, and A. D. Martin. 2002. Adherence to exercise prescriptions: Effects of prescribing moderate versus higher levels of intensity and frequency. *Health Psychology* 21(5):452–58.

Peterson, C. 2000. The future of optimism. *American Psychologist* 55(1):44–55.

Peterson, C., and L. C. Barrett. 1987. Explanatory style and academic performance among university freshmen. *Journal of Personality and Social Psychology* 53(3):603–7.

Peterson, C., and M. E. P. Seligman. 1984. Causal explanations as a risk factor for depression: Theory and evidence. *Psychological Review* 91:347–74.

———. 2004. *Character Strengths and Virtues: A Handbook and Classification.* New York: Oxford University Press.

Poloma, M. M., and B. F. Pendleton. 1991. The effects of prayer and prayer experiences on measures of general well-being. *Journal of Psychology and Theology* 19(1):71–83.

Pressman, S. D., S. Cohen, G. E. Miller, A. Barkin, B. S. Rabin, and J. J. Treanor. 2005. Loneliness, social network size, and immune response to influenza vaccination in college freshmen. *Health Psychology* 24(3):297–306.

Robles, T. F., and J. K. Kiecolt-Glaser. 2003. The physiology of marriage: Pathways to health. *Physiology and Behavior* 79:409–16.

Rosmond, R., M. F. Dallman, and P. Björntorp. 1998. Stress-related cortisol secretion in men: Relationships with abdominal obesity and endocrine, metabolic, and hemodynamic abnormalities. *Journal of Clinical Endocrinology and Metabolism* 83(6):1853–59.

Rossi, P., G. I. Andriesse, P. L. Oey, G. H. Wieneke, J. M. Roelofs, and L. M. Akkermans. 1998. Stomach distension increases efferent muscle sympathetic nerve activity and blood pressure in healthy humans. *Journal of Neurological Sciences* 161(2): 148–55.

Roth, B., and T. Stanley. 2002. Mindfulness-based stress reduction and healthcare utilization in the inner city: Preliminary findings. *Alternative Therapies* 8(1):60–66.

Roth, D. L., and D. S. Holmes. 1985. Influence of physical fitness in determining the impact of stressful life events on physical and psychologic health. *Psychosomatic Medicine* 47(2): 164–73.

Roth, S., and L. J. Cohen. 1986. Approach, avoidance, and coping with stress. *American Psychologist* 41:813–19.

Santos, J., and M. H. Perdue. 2000. Stress and neuroimmune regulation of gut mucosal function. *Gut* 47(suppl. IV): iv49–iv51.

Sapolsky, R. M. 2004. *Why Zebras Don't Get Ulcers.* New York: Henry Holt and Company.

Sarno, J. 1998. *The Mindbody Prescription: Healing the Body, Healing the Pain.* New York: Warner Books.

Satterfield, J. M. 2001. Happiness, excellence, and optimal human functioning. *Western Journal of Medicine* 173:26–29.

Schneider, R. H., F. Staggers, C. N. Alexander, W. Sheppard, M. Rainforth, and K. Kondwani. 1995. A randomized controlled trial of stress reduction for hypertension in older African Americans. *Hypertension* 26:820–27.

Schwartz, A. R., W. Gerin, K. W. Davidson, T. G. Pickering, J. F. Brosschot, J. F. Thayer, N. Christenfeld, and W. Linden. 2003. Toward a causal model of cardiovascular responses to stress and the development of cardiovascular disease. *Psychosomatic Medicine* 65:22–35.

Seeman, T. E., L. F. Dubin, and M. Seeman. 2003. Religiosity/spirituality and health: A critical review of the evidence for biological pathways. *American Psychologist* 58(1):53–63.

Segerstrom, S. C., S. E. Taylor, M. E. Kemeny, and J. L. Fahey. 1998. Optimism is associated with mood, coping, and immune change in response to stress. *Journal of Personality and Social Psychology* 74(6):1646–55.

Seligman, M. E. P. 2002. *Authentic Happiness: Using the New Positive Psychology to Realize Your Potential for Lasting Fulfillment.* New York: Free Press.

Seligman, M. E. P., T. A. Steen, N. Park, and C. Peterson. 2005. Positive psychology progress: Empirical validation of interventions. *American Psychologist* 60(5):410–21.

Sies, H., W. Stahl, and A. Sevanian. 2005. Nutritional, dietary, and postprandial oxidative stress. *Journal of Nutrition* 135:969–72.

Sloan, D. M. 2004. Emotion regulation in action: Emotional reactivity in experiential avoidance. *Behaviour Research and Therapy* 42:1257–70.

Sloan, D. M., B. P. Marx, and E. M. Epstein. 2005. Further examination of the exposure model underlying the efficacy of written emotional disclosure. *Journal of Consulting and Clinical Psychology* 73:549–54.

Smyth, J. M., A. A. Stone, A. Hurewitz, and A. Kaell. 1999. Effects of writing about stressful experiences on symptom reduction in patients with asthma or rheumatoid arthritis: A randomized trial. *Journal of the American Medical Association* 281:1304–9.

Southwick, W. M., J. D. Bremner, A. Rasmusson, C. A. Morgan, A. Arnsten, and D. S. Charney. 1999. Role of norepinephrine in the pathophysiology and treatment of post-traumatic stress disorder. *Biological Psychiatry* 46:1192–1204.

Syrjala, K., C. Cummings, and G. Donaldson. 1992. Hypnosis or cognitive behavioral training for the reductions of pain and nausea during cancer treatment: A controlled clinical trial. *Pain* 48:137–46.

Taylor, S. E., M. E. Kemeny, G. M. Reed, J. E. Bower, and T. L. Gruenewald. 2000. Psychological resources, positive illusions, and health. *American Psychologist* 55(1):99–109.

Temoshok, L. 1987. Personality, coping style, emotion, and cancer: Towards an integrative model. *Cancer Surveys* 6(3):545–67.

Thompson, S. C. 1985. Finding positive meaning in a stressful event and coping. *Basic and Applied Social Psychology* 6(4):279–95.

Uchino, B. N., J. T. Cacioppo, and J. K. Kiecolt-Glaser. 1996. The relationship between social support and physiological processes: A review with emphasis on underlying mechanisms and implications for health. *Psychological Bulletin* 119(3):488–531.

United States Department of Health and Human Services and United States Department of Agriculture. 2005. Dietary Guidelines for Americans: 2005. Washington, DC: United States Department of Health and Human Services.

Van Eck, M., H. Berkhof, N. Nicolson, and J. Sulon. 1996. The effects of perceived stress, traits, mood states, and stressful daily events on salivary cortisol. *Psychosomatic Medicine* 58:447–58.

Vicennati, V., L. Ceroni, L. Gagliardi, A. Gambineri, and R. Pasquali. 2002. Response of the hypothalamic-pituitary-adrenocortical axis to high-protein/fat and high-carbohydrate meals in women with different obesity phenotypes. *Journal of Clinical Endocrinology and Metabolism* 87(8):3984–88.

Waldfogel, S. 1997. Spirituality in medicine. *Primary Care* 24(4): 963–76.

Walker, L. G., M. B. Walker, K. Ogston, S. D. Heys, A. K. Ah-See, I. D. Miller, A. W. Hutcheon, T. K. Sarkar, and O. Eremin. 1999. Psychological, clinical, and pathological effects of relaxation training and guided imagery during primary chemotherapy. *British Journal of Cancer* 80:262–68.

Wenzel, L., K. Glanz, and C. Lerman. 2002. Stress, coping, and health behavior. In *Health Behavior and Health Education: Theory, Research, and Practice*, edited by K. Glanz, B. Rimer, and F. Lewis. San Francisco: Jossey-Bass.

Wink, P., and M. Dillon. 2003. Religiousness, spirituality, and psychosocial functioning in late adulthood: Findings from a longitudinal study. *Psychology and Aging* 18(4):916–24.

Yanovski, S. 2003. Sugar and fat: Cravings and aversions. *Journal of Nutrition* 133:835S–837S.

Young, L. R., and M. Nestle. 2002. The contribution of expanding portion sizes to the U.S. obesity epidemic. *American Journal of Public Health* 92(2):246–49.

Claire Michaels Wheeler, MD, Ph.D., worked as an emergency medicine physician before she took a Ph.D. in psychology at the University of Michigan. There, she codirected a long-term study of the emotional and psychological consequences of severe injuries. She is the founder of Mind-Body Medicine of Portland, a provider of workshops, classes, and seminars on mind-body health and creativity. Dr. Michaels is an instructor at Portland State University's School of Community Health, as well as a core faculty member for the Center for Mind-Body Medicine in Washington, DC. She was key personnel on a grant provided by the NIH to Oregon Health and Science University for the integration of mind-body medicine and other integrative medicine approaches into the medical and nursing school curricula, and she participated in a series of CAM grand rounds, instructing physicians and medical students in the clinical application of mind-body medicine. Dr. Wheeler lives in Portland, OR.

more **simple solutions** to real challenges
from new**harbinger**publications